How to Manage Children's Challenging Behaviour

Edited by
Bill Rogers

Paul Chapman Publishing

Paul Chapman Publishing
A SAGE Publications Company
1 Oliver's Yard
55 City Road
London EC1Y 1SP

SAGE Publications Inc
2455 Teller Road
Thousand Oaks, California 91320

Sage Publications India Pvt Ltd
B-42, Panchsheel Enclave
Post Box 4109
New Delhi 110 017

Library of Congress Control Number: 2004090752

A catalogue record for this book is available from the British Library

ISBN 1 4129 0216 9
ISBN 1 4129 0217 7 (pbk)

Typeset by Pantek Arts Ltd
Printed in Great Britain by Cromwell Press Ltd, Trowbridge, Wiltshire

Contents

Acknowledgements

To all my colleagues who have taken time to share their stories; for their honesty, commitment and patient goodwill recounted here.

This is their book.

These are their children, their students.

My thanks to my colleagues at Griffith University, particularly Dr Bette Blance, Dr Alan Edwards and Professor Neil Russell who have supported this project from the outset.

To my colleagues at Sage Publications who have encouraged me in this project, particularly Marianne Lagrange and Joyce Lynch.

To Felicia Schmidt for taking on another pressured typing task – thanks again.

To my family Lora, Elizabeth and Sarah – as ever – many thanks.

Bill Rogers

Contributors

Some of the contributors in this book have preferred not to name their school for natural reasons of ethical probity. The names of individual children in each account have been changed for the same reason.

Debbie Hoy is the principal of an infant school near London. Debbie has also had wide experience consulting to schools in the area of behaviour management and supporting children with special needs.

Dr Bette Blance heads up a professional development team (Bette Blance and Associates) in New Zealand. Previously Bette has been a school principal and was (until recently) Associate Director of the Centre for Professional Development at Griffith University (Australia).

Pamela Curtain is a primary teacher and an education consultant currently supporting schools in Queensland.

Mara Smart is the deputy principal of Musgrave Hill State School, Queensland. Mara was formerly a Behaviour Advisory Teacher.

Mariette West is a teacher at Musgrave Hill State School, Queensland. Mariette, Pamela and Mara have developed a number of behaviour management plans for children with special needs and behaviour disorders.

Peter D'Angelo is an experienced secondary English teacher. A migrant to Australia he has always worked in school settings with high multicultural populations. He is also a poet and has had several books of poetry published. Peter's essays are courtesy of *Education Quarterly Australia* (many thanks to Kathy Skelton) and *The Age* newspaper (Melbourne) – and, in particular, thanks to Larry Schwartz for his support.

Ros Daniels is a senior primary school teacher who has worked in schools in southern England. Ros has also been an education consultant to schools in the area of behaviour management and discipline.

Patsy Finger is a senior primary school teacher currently teaching in Queensland. Patsy has developed a number of initiatives in the area of behaviour support.

Heather Fraser is an experienced primary school teacher. She has taught widely (particularly in country Victoria).

Denise Frost is an experienced primary school teacher currently teaching in Tasmania.

Sharn Hatch has been a practising teacher both in Australia and overseas. At present, Sharn works as an associate lecturer at Griffith University, Queensland. She teaches in the Faculty of Education in the areas of educational psychology, sociology and communication. Her area of interest is concerned with young people's conceptualisations of the future and the cultural realities they appropriate to formulate those visions of the future.

Karen Kearney is a 'beginning' (mature age) teacher in Queensland. Karen also has been a member of the Australian army and police force. She has worked with young people in Police-Citizens' Youth Clubs and believes sport can be a key tool in educational outcomes.

Elizabeth McPherson (née Rogers) has taught for the last three years – as an infant teacher – in Melbourne. She is currently on leave, mother to a beautiful (newly arrived) first child (a daughter). She still teaches one day a week.

Kerrie Miller is an experienced integration teacher currently working in country Victoria. Kerrie works with a wide range of children with special needs.

Carmen Price is a behaviour management psychologist of many years experience and works – widely – with schools in Queensland.

Bill Rogers (editor and contributor) has been an education consultant for the last 15 years and is currently an Adjunct Professor (Education) at Griffith University, Queensland, Australia.

Carmel Ryan is the deputy principal of Labrador State School in Queensland. Carmel and her colleagues have developed a whole-school model for behaviour and learning; a project. Their approach emphases the concept of a 'peaceable school', emphasising problem-solving, mediation and resolving issues of concern.

Ken Sell is an experienced teacher of over 15 years. For the last three years he has been working as an Advisory Support Teacher for Education Queensland in the Nambour District on the Sunshine Coast. He has designed and implemented many in-service workshops relevant to primary and secondary teachers as well as advising administrators in areas of social equity and the interpersonal dynamics found within schools. Ken is presently finishing a research project relating to his work in schools.

Larry Taylor has, over 30 years, worked in schools as a classroom teacher with Years 2 to 7, as an educational advisor in effective learning and teaching, and as a learning support and learning technology teacher. He has accreditation in the Myers-Briggs personality type indicator and Dr William Glasser's 'Choice Theory'.

Leanne Wright is an experienced secondary teacher (in Tasmania) currently supporting schools in the area of consultancy in behaviour management, student welfare and discipline.

A teacher's response has crucial consequences …
it creates a climate of compliance or defiance, a mood
of contentment or contention, a desire to make amends
or to take revenge …

Teachers have the power to affect a child's life for better
or worse. A child becomes what he/she experiences.
While parents possess the original key to their offspring's
experience, teachers have a spare key.

They, too, can open or close the minds and hearts of children.

Haim Ginott (1972)

In the morning when you rise unwillingly let this thought be
present – I am rising to the work of a human being.

Marcus Aurelius (*The Meditations of Marcus Aurelius V*)

All royalties from the sale of this book
are donated to the charity *World Vision*
for children's education programmes
in South East Asia.

Introduction

Bill Rogers

This book came about as a result of working directly alongside teachers working with challenging children and children with emotional behavioural disorders. My colleagues and I believe that these accounts deserve a much wider audience. The direct, practical and positive nature of these accounts will immediately resonate with teachers.

These teachers (from Australia and the UK) work with children in mainstream and special education settings. I have worked with some of them as a mentor teacher, others I know within my role as Adjunct Professor of Education at Griffith University. These accounts range across primary and secondary school settings; from individual children with challenging behaviour including children with emotional and behavioural disorder (EBD) through to whole class settings where challenging and problem behaviour has been effectively addressed by these teachers.

Teachers spend a third of their waking and working day with children. Most teachers in most schools on most days engage students in their learning with effort, energy and goodwill. Many teachers have a passion for making a difference – even a 'deceptively small' difference in children's lives. Their goodwill, energy and patience is sometimes stretched 'to the limit' by some of the children they are called to teach, 'manage' and support. Some of the children we read of in these accounts are children whose family dynamic does not always support what schools seek to be and do. The 'causative pathology' of some of these children is disturbing – even dysfunctional – yet these teachers never 're-victimise' a child by saying, 'What can we do with him? What can we expect? Look where he comes from …!' While these teachers know that there are many factors that affect a child's behaviour (and learning potential) they also know that *behaviour is also developed, and learned, in context*. The context of the school can make a significant difference, as these accounts testify.

All the teachers who have written here believe that they can, and will, make a difference in the lives of 'their' children.

I am frequently encouraged by the incredible moral energy of the sort demonstrated and lived out by these teachers. In sharing their experiences more widely I trust you, too, will be encouraged. These teachers have made a difference – a significant difference at times – to the lives of their children. These teachers remind us of what we went into teaching for.

The teachers who have written in this book have shared not just 'accounts' of their children – their teaching and management – they have shared themselves with us. Their honesty, their goodwill, their courage, their passion for what they do (and why) comes across clearly to us. The 'immediacy' of these 'stories' creates that common bond we have with our colleagues.

These narratives are, at times, intensely personal and moving. My colleagues have all indicated that they share these accounts – these 'narratives' – to remind each other of our common struggle yet also to identify our shared journey, our shared hopes and to celebrate our profession. I wish these accounts could be read more widely by the general public so they – too – could more consciously celebrate our profession. At least the parents of the children recounted here know these teachers made a difference.

All teachers, at every level in a school, face similar issues of behaviour, from the typical calling out, butting in, inappropriate loudness (in a very small room) through to the more disturbing issues of bullying, violence and behaviour disorders. Every teacher has also had to address the question of how to meaningfully and realistically support that small percentage of students who present with emotional and behavioural disorders. This 'small' percentage – one to five per cent in most schools (Rogers, 2003) – have the potential to 'eat up' a lot of teacher time and energy, effort and goodwill. These teachers, and the schools in which they were supported, share the realistic and practical measures they took to support these children.

This book addresses the issue of challenging behaviours and behaviour disorders in schools and how teachers – in a supportive collegial team – have made a significant difference to their students. They have made a direct difference in terms of the students' behaviour, attitude, self-esteem and peer acceptance.

Later in this book Sharn Hatch shares how such narratives can be understood, celebrated and used in our professional journey. She notes that:

> *Narratives are active and not just passive retelling of events gone by. They are a way of making meaning out of the experiences of (our) everyday life; of visualising the world, organising the past and explaining the present. They help us identify, create and justify our place in the world.* (Chapter 7)

At all times my colleagues have been sensitive to the ethical probity involved in such narrative writing. Names of children have been changed, and no school (as such) is identified.

As much as possible, I have tried to let my colleagues share their own story; to let their voice engage the central learnings we can all draw from these accounts. At the beginning of each chapter I have sought to outline the key aspects of behaviour leadership being addressed. In Chapter 6 I have drawn together the key principles of behaviour leadership that clearly emerge from their work with children.

I have been encouraged by these narratives of my colleagues. I hope you, too, will be similarly encouraged to 'make a difference' with the students you encounter.

1

Emotional and Behavioural Disorder: the Challenge to Our Thinking, Attitudes and Strategy

We cannot predict where our students may end up

Bill Rogers

Some teachers get into a habit of predicting what will happen to 'their charges' – where they'll probably 'end up'. 'He'll never get anywhere, he's lazy, slow, doesn't concentrate, doesn't apply himself ...' 'He's so stupid ...' 'He'll never amount to anything.' 'He'll probably send up in jail ...' . I had a few teachers who told me I'd 'never amount to anything' – they were right (just joking).

When we struggle to make sense of children's behaviour – in a school context – it can be tempting to make easy judgements about their future. I have done it myself as a teacher. In reflecting on the many challenging students I've worked with I've predicted and been proved wrong. The issue is not whether we are 'right' or 'wrong' in our predictions but that predicting – as such – is unhelpful. Like the well known 'expectancy effect' (Rosenthal, 1986) it can unwittingly affect our relationship and our directed beliefs about how effectively we can work with the student in their learning and behaviour.

These four essays describe how teachers reflect on such predictive teacher behaviour and the effect it can have on their students' learning and behaviour.

I had some strange teachers in the 1950s in post-war Britain. It was a different time, a different society with different hierarchies and social structure. Authority – particularly at school – was rarely questioned (at least by 'pupils'). If I 'chatted' in class or spoke while the teacher was teaching I had chalk thrown at me, was verbally chastised many times, got a 'thick ear' or had to do detention. Talking while the teacher was talking was considered a serious dis-ruptive behaviour for some teachers. On one such occasion (when I was 14) a teacher strode over to my desk and jabbed my shoulder with a vigorous, kinaesthetic finger, demanding to know if I was 'brought up or dragged up' (in reference to my chatting quietly to my mate during 'class instruction'). I can still hear the words. It was the only occasion when I directly, and physically, stood up to a teacher. I stood up and – facing him – said, 'It's none of your bloody business.' No teacher was going to have a go at my parents! I walked out of the classroom to a stunned silence – my heart thumping. I went home. I was the 'Trojan horse' for the class group. Even then (1960) I think he realised he'd gone too far.

I 'answered teachers back' on other occasions – mostly I got detentions; on other occasions I got the cane. I once got caned (hands and back of leg) from the headmaster for breaking a pencil which a student had initially snatched from me. The principal (supervising our class) had only seen me; he miscued, mistarget-ted and I had 'argued' and 'answered back' to him and was consequently 'rude'. I got the cane. No right of reply in those days. This same principal once ear-pulled me so badly he scored a nail print that drew blood at the back of my ear – ouch! It was the only occasion my mother went to the school in my 'defence' – she was magnificent as she told him what she would do if he ever laid his hands on me again. He apologised (reluctantly), becoming annoyingly sycophantic the following day.

It is interesting – in forgiving retrospect – to wonder what I would do as a teacher in similar situations to those of my teachers in the 50s and early 60s. I know what I would not do. I wouldn't make a student move briskly up and down three flights of stairs as a punishment for not paying attention in science class and 'being *stupid*' with weights and pulleys – 'a little unthinking perhaps, hard-ly stupid, Mr Siddons' – 'Don't answer back, Rogers. Take those 4 lb weights' (one in each hand, they had rings on their semi-pyramidal structures) 'and walk briskly up and down' (three flights of stairs) 'and then report straight back here to me!' All of this (of course) in front of fellow students who – in part – grinned and who – in part – were glad it wasn't them!

Once outside the classroom I went and sat at the bottom of the stairs for five minutes or so. I came back into the class feigning breathlessness. (Was he *really* so stupid in thinking I'd actually carry weights up three flights of stairs?! Apparently he believed I was that 'biddable'.) 'Now will you learn?! Let that be a lesson to you.' He berated me in front of my peers. I gave a suitable – demure – 'I-have-learned' look and went back to the entrails of my weights and pulleys experiment.

MY 'CHALLENGING BEHAVIOUR'

Two days before I left high school in 1961 (summer term in Great Britain) I went to school half an hour earlier than normal; secreted under my jumper was a large painting on oil paper. It illustrated a portrait of my science teacher surrounded by several other luminaries (portraits of teachers I didn't like). It was painted after the manner of Salvador Dali, the Spanish surrealist painter. Dali was (apparently) inspired by Freudian theories of the unconscious. I didn't know this at the time but I had read of his work (at the library) and been inspired by his 'melting', surrealist imagery. It took me a few weeks to get the painting 'right'. I'm colour blind so the colours must have looked interesting.

On the day in question I arrived early at school, complete with sturdy drawing pins and, alone, I pinned it on the large notice board just inside the double doors – at least I thought I was alone. A prefect had espied me. In those days, some prefects were like quasi police. He reported me.

At morning form assembly Mr Siddons (my form master and discipline master – his title) held up my unsigned picture. 'This is yours, is it not, Rogers?' I didn't deny it – I was rather proud of it, only I hadn't planned *this* kind of exposure. 'You know what's going to happen to you, don't you?' Suitably mollified I said 'Yes'. 'Lunchtime – my office.' I sighed – the cane again, and just two days before the end of term. As he dismissed us I saw him take the rolled up painting into his office, close the door and walk off. I surreptitiously sneaked in after he had gone, retrieved my property and waited for a suitable moment before period 1 to put it back on the notice board. I then hot-footed it up to Level 3 to the double classroom to watch a black and white film, *Otters in Canada* (or something similar). It was an end of term 'filler' taken – no doubt – by a teacher dreaming of his summer holidays and partial freedom (as I would many years later when I became a teacher).

Mr Siddons, of course, found out all too soon about this dastardly, anarchic act. He was – apparently – livid. He sent a prefect to ferret me out. I was sitting with the Form 4 students in the darkened double classroom while the 16mm film reels clicked on … A loud knock on the classroom door, a narrow band of light fell across the darkened room and a voice squeaked out 'Is Billy Rogers, 4C, here?' 'Who?' The teacher sounded barely interested. The student went on – 'Mr Siddons wants to see him immediately.' Maybe the student messenger didn't sound urgent enough – the supervising teacher said 'I'll send him as soon as the film's finished, don't worry.'

Back in the darkness, with distracting otters (or was it beavers?), I quickly planned my getaway. I whispered to my mate, 'I'm off – don't tell them I've gone.' I sneaked out, arms feeling for the wall; I inched my back along the wall towards the door and found freedom. I had seen many black and white films of military men in *Stalag 137* (whatever), *The Wooden Horse* and *The Colditz Story*. I often imagined myself as the head of the 'escape committee' at school. I was now 'on the run'. I raced downstairs on tip-toe (not easy), grabbed bag, gear and coat and made my way out the rear entrance of the school to avoid capture. I ran home. Later that day I told my mum and dad. My dad wisely – and helpfully – asked me what I wanted to do about 'it all'. I told him that I didn't want to go back to *that* school. We were not on the phone at home so the school could not reach us quickly. We got the statutory letter some days later, 'We are extremely disappointed, …' (etc.) I went to another school for almost 12 months and then we emigrated to Australia – as a family – for the princely sum of ten English pounds. It was well worth it.

TEACHERS WHO BELIEVED IN ME

There were – thankfully – kind, generous, caring, motivational teachers at that school. I remember my art teacher with flowing cape, ambiguous perfume (from under the cape), flowing chestnut locks (the Lady of Shallot?). We were early – and confusingly – entranced by Mrs Hart, then highly respectful of this talented and motivational teacher. She enrolled me in a national art exam. I complained I couldn't do it because I was badly colour blind. She believed in me, however, and encouraged me and supported me to 'go for it'. I did a painting of 'Men Trawling in the North Sea' (a set topic choice). I had painted them straining at nets, on a bucking trawler in a rough sea. I had apparently painted the men with green hair, and strangely coloured Anglo-Saxon skin (puce?). I think I got the sou-westers an acceptable yellow or orangey colour. I received no placing in the exam but I got a beautiful, embossed (national) certificate that I was so proud of. My confidence in drawing and art owes much to Mrs Hart.

I had a few other teachers who believed in me, like Mr Randall my English teacher, who was most supportive of my writing, particularly my Dickens essays. He always treated me with courtesy and respect, and addressed the 'emergent adult' in me. I remember these teachers with affection – some teachers make a difference in your life.

So, I left school at 15, a migrant to Australia with mixed memories of school. I worked on building sites in Queensland. I had a brief stint in the army (artillery, national service). I became a teacher later in life (as a mature age learner), having also been a carpenter, an architectural draughtsman, a young parish minister (seven years) and then a teacher, consultant, university lecturer and professor.

THE MORAL OF THE STORY

We cannot predict (nor is it worth predicting) what will happen to our students. We are better served working with, encouraging and supporting our students for the short time they are with us.

It is also worth remembering that learning is life-long; it doesn't begin, or end, with formal schooling. Some of my teachers taught me how *not* to teach and how *not* to manage and discipline students. Others gave me sufficient messages of hope, confidence and encouragement to make the choices that have helped form my on-going educational journey. I wish I could share that with Mrs Hart and Mr Randall.

Teach; encourage a student's potential and hopeful tomorrow – don't predict.

The 'Pygmalion effect': where expectancy can lead

Bill Rogers

There is a story in classical mythology where Pygmalion, the sculptor, spends his days on the island of Cyprus creating a beautiful female statue. The myth doesn't say he was dimwitted, it simply records that he 'fell in love' with it and earnestly prayed to Venus to bring the statue to life. He married the former statue .... love bore fruit .... (sounds like a bad American soap, doesn't it?). Bernard Shaw took the myth further.

In 1914 George Bernard Shaw's play Pygmalion was performed in London. Among other things his story demonstrated that what one believes, attributes and communicates to another person can have a profound effect in terms of self-belief and behaviour change of that person. The professor of linguistics has a bet with a friend (the Colonel) that given sufficient time he can train a 'mere' Cockney flower girl to pass for a 'real lady'. Eliza the flower girl is treated quite differently by the professor of linguistics and the Colonel. Eliza says:

> *'.... the difference between a lady and a flower girl is not how she behaves, but how she's treated. I shall always be a flower girl to Professor Higgins, because he always treats me as a flower girl, and always will; but I know I can be a lady to you, because you always treat me as a lady, and always will.'*

Perhaps the message of the play is that our expectations may determine more than we realise. It may not always be the other person who is the problem.

Back in 1963 the psychologist Robert Rosenthal and his colleagues set up experiments to test what is sometimes called the 'expectancy effect' or 'self-fulfilling prophecy'. Randomly assigned rats were divided into two groups termed 'maze-bright' and 'maze-dull'. College undergraduates who tested the rats on maze trials only knew their rat sample as 'bright' or 'dull'. Ten trials later (over five consecutive days) the results indicated that the 'bright' rats nearly doubled the 'dull' rats in maze performances. Rosenthal concluded that rather than any real 'intelligence' differences increasing the score of the 'bright' rats, it was the expectations of the experimenters communicated via tactile and kinetic cues that had an effect on rat performance.

This 'effect' has been widely studied with child and teacher relationships in classroom settings. Would randomly assigned children, identified only as 'dull' or 'bright', exhibit similar differences? That 'painful and dull grade', those 'swines' in grade 6, contrasted with the really 'bright grade'. 'You're a lucky so and so, they're the best lot in our school ....', 'I had that group and they're marvellous ....' 'That group in grade 5, they're very bright, you know ....' Would such labelled associations present a similar picture, and outcome, to the tests of Rosenthal? Evidently yes. Rosenthal and Jacobsen wrote about their research in schools and titled their work *Pygmalion in the Classroom*.

If we characteristically think of a particular grade (or group of students) as a 'pain', 'hopeless' or 'never-amount-to-anything'; if we assign them to a mental slag heap; if we expect them (or particular individuals) to fail, be a pest or 'drive us up the wall'; if we expect them to perform to the badinage of staff room gossip .... we might find our expectations working as a self-fulfilling prophecy. I have worked with colleagues who have described, even defined, a group of students as 'them' in contrast to 'us': 'I've got to win here; I've got to prove that I'm the boss.' I've even heard teachers describe a class (with admittedly challenging students) as 'the enemy'. It is not even a contest, let alone a 'war'. There are teachers who will communicate their expectations through consequent behaviour as if students are an 'enemy' – a recipe for conflict.

Of course student behaviour can be extremely difficult, challenging and stressful at times. What my colleagues and I have learned is that colleague support is crucial in helping one to cope, understand, address and manage such behaviours. Importantly, our colleagues are a critical resource for the development of school-wide strategies, plans and programmes, necessary when managing and supporting challenging student behaviours. When teachers lapse into such negative descriptors it is – mostly – out of intense (often unrelieved) frustration.

In classes in the more 'challenging schools' (as they are often described in 'teacher shorthand') 60 or 70 per cent of students are basically co-operative, considerate, responsible and mostly amenable to positive, respectful and confident teacher leadership. Between 15 and 20 per cent (broad by distributive percentages) are the students who tend to behave in attentional and distracting ways. Some behave in more challenging ways that exhibit a miscue of 'power' ('I can do what I want and no one can really stop me!') These students will often exhibit such behaviours in the first meetings over the first few weeks. Often many of these students can be supportively encouraged, within confident teacher leadership, to work with shared and fair rights and responsibilities. (See later, p 56) A much smaller percentage (one to five per cent) present with emotional and behavioural disorders.

The more we expect (think, believe, attribute) particular students, or even a whole class, to be difficult – even impossible – to teach or manage, the more we may unintentionally communicate bad behaviour traits to Johnny, or to his class group. Our prophecy may seem as if it is fulfilled. 'I knew he'd bomb out – he *always* does ....!' 'I knew they'd upset me, they *always* upset me.'

Listening to staff room gossip – 'Oh no! I've got those b......s in 9C again!', 'He's a real little sh-t', '8D are such a pack of animals!' – one wonders how much some teachers telegraph the attribute of 'sh-tness' to the children, or class, they teach.

Did your parents ever say, 'You're *just* like your father .... he *always* leaves his clothes around', 'Lazy .... *just* like your brother', 'You *never* do what I ask', 'You *always* whine', 'Why don't you ever concentrate?!', '*How many times* have I told you!?', 'Don't you *ever* listen?', 'Look!! You *should* be able to do that maths *by now*!'. If children hear this kind of language frequently it will have an effect, but it may not be the 'wake-up' effect some adults expect. Even if our global attributions are partly true, stating them frequently will unnecessarily reinforce the self-defeating expectations.

The 'Pygmalion effect' thrives on hyperbole and the global misconception that says behaviour and person are equivalent – or that things, people, relationships have an inevitable 'mustness' about them. 'This kid *must* be difficult because his mother is ..., his father has just "shot through" and he lives in those awful flats ... and there's substance abuse and ...' or 'We *can't* expect much more from him because of his home life ...' Further, such negative expectancy may significantly affect the realistic support we can give, and the difference we can make, to students whose home lives and circumstances are disturbing and dysfunctional (Rogers, 2003).

We can communicate expectation in a variety of ways, but we know, from our own childhood, adolescence and adulthood, when somebody is telegraphing inadequacy, failure, incompetence or easy judgement.

CASE EXAMPLE (TED)

Ted was 'dumped' in my class because the grade 6 teacher couldn't cope (sorry, he was 'placed' in my class). I was told he was 'totally disruptive', 'dirty', 'unreliable', 'never listens', 'grossly untidy work', etc. Outwardly Ted looked like the young children sometimes displayed on Salvation Army posters. He boldly asserted that he was 'tough' and the first day was overly disruptive (attention-seeking, loud, verbally rude). Any work he handed in looked like it had been used as a towel after a footy game.

After a month, things began to change. No magic formulas. I accepted his work as it was (he especially enjoyed maths) and commented clearly and specifically only on correct work, and attempts at achieving correct work. 'Good on you Ted; the way you worked those fractions out was spot-on, different from the way we set it out on the board and easier too'. I ignored the scribble over his decimal fractions, the many dirty thumbprints (he learned, later, to wash his hands).

Whenever he evidenced co-operative behaviour he was affirmed; specifically and often quietly (and one to one) so as not to unnecessarily embarrass him. 'Thanks Ted for helping Maria and sharing your ideas ....' 'You were co-operative when ...' When he was disruptive, affecting other students' rights, he was dealt with calmly, consistently and, at times, quite firmly with appropriate consequences for his disruptive behaviour. I *expected* Ted to develop positive learning and behaviour. It wasn't easy. I always followed up with a quiet chat – away from the other students – in 'non-contact' time (Rogers, 1998). Day by day I saw small changes in Ted's attitude to learning, his overall behaviour and his relations with other students.

Near the close of term (and parent-teacher night) he came up, crooked his arm around my neck and said, 'You're OK.' 'Thanks Ted,' I replied (nursing my neck), 'so are you.'

His mother, who had missed other parent-teacher nights (who wants to listen to bad news all the time?) actually came along on this night. The first thing I did was to ask her if she'd like a cup of tea. Well, she was a bit hostile and just sat upright, frowning, refused the tea and waited for the regular reportage. I said, 'Mrs _____, thanks for coming, it's been a pleasure to have Ted here this term. His maths work has always been completed with effort and skill' (I didn't tell her about the dirty thumb prints) 'and he really gets on well with other children in the class' (I didn't tell her about the first four weeks). I showed her examples of Ted's work, describing his effort, his energy, his growing confidence. Her eyes nearly fell out and she said, 'That's the first time I've ever heard Ted spoken about like that ... that's why I came up. He said the teacher (I mean you) said how pleased he was with his maths and that and I couldn't believe it.' She left with a big smile, a hearty thanks and 'Oh, Mr Rogers, he's washing a lot now ...'

Ted left a few weeks before Christmas (before the rest of the class). He was moving to another part of Australia. He came up to me the day before he left school, drew me aside and asked me if I liked lobster. 'Love it!' (I was a bit surprised by the question.) He turned up the day before he left, combed hair (same jeans and jumper), twinkle in his eye and handed me a dampish bundle wrapped in Christmas paper. It was a lobster. I thanked him (I do like lobster). However, when I cracked it open, later at home, well ... it sort of smelt. I gave it to the cat. Ted, if you read this, no offence mate, I probably left it too long in the sun. (Ted would be nearly 30 now.)

'Dear Luke': what I saw at the outset and how children's behaviour challenges us in positive ways

Elizabeth McPherson

Elizabeth McPherson (née Rogers) is in her second year of teaching. As a primary school teacher (infants) she has come across the widest range of behaviour, needs and backgrounds in her students. In this account Elizabeth shares a letter she wrote to one of her students at the close of her first year of teaching. Luke is a little boy who made a significant impact on her life (as she did in his). She has asked his mother to pass it on to Luke when he starts high school. Luke's mother really appreciated the letter.

This letter clearly illustrates how a child's first perceptions of school can affect their behaviour and the difference a teacher's perception can have on how challenging behaviour can be positively addressed.

This article was first published in Classroom Magazine (May, 2002).

Dear Luke,
When I first met you, day one, you were clinging to your mother's skirt; I had never seen a five year old so small. You must have been only 70 centimetres high, how big the school must have seemed.

When your mother finally summoned the courage to leave, you hid under the tables. Despite my best efforts I couldn't persuade you to come out and join the rest of the grade. When I still hadn't coaxed you out two days later, I approached your mum. 'What should I do, he won't join in with anything?' I asked. 'Shall I leave him till he's ready or force him to join in?' Your mum began to cry, she said she just wanted everything to be perfect for you. You're very fortunate that she loves you so much; some of the other children in our class aren't so lucky. I wanted everything to be perfect too and already in my first week of teaching, I felt like I was failing two people.

It took your mum and dad a few days to decide what they wanted me to do, and in the end they asked me to leave you until you were ready. I asked the other children not to fuss over you when you were hiding under the classroom furniture, funnily enough they were happy just to let you be. Plenty of them were probably feeling scared too; maybe they wished that they'd thought of your approach to school. Some recesses I didn't get a break, I didn't want to leave you alone in the classroom, but then most of

9

the time you would come out to playground duty with me and follow at a distance.

It must have been difficult for you, not knowing what to do at school; sometimes it was a bit difficult and scary for me too. Like your mum, I wanted my whole class to have a perfect start to school life. But I guess with people there's no such thing as perfection.

On the day of our first assembly, we lined up and rushed over to the hall. You were really scared, this was new for you, and I'd forgotten to explain to you what was going on; I was cross at myself. You taught me my first and most valuable rule when teaching grade preps (infants) – explain every detail and role-play new situations!

When we started going to specialist classes, you got very nervous. You told me you hated the library teacher, the art and music teacher and the Italian teacher, you said you wanted to stay with me. A light bulb suddenly switched on in the cavernous recesses of my mind – you were scared of everyone – except me. I began to realise that I was special to you and you were special to me.

I remember, only too well, the day one of our 'more challenging' class members nearly cut your finger off with some scissors. I was helping someone on a computer and when I turned around, I saw you clutching your hand and you were dripping with blood. It's funny the way people react in situations like that. All I could think of, Luke, was making it all right for you… I scooped you up and carried you to the sick bay, while the principal minded the rest of the grade. You were sobbing and I had blood dripping down my arms and legs and smeared on my face – we must have looked a sight. You were so brave, even when the school secretary called your mum you decided to stick it out until the end of the day. I remember you asked me 'Why do we have to have naughty boys in our class?' I didn't know what to say, my heart was breaking for you. How could I explain that I didn't want the 'naughty' boys to be there any more than you did?

I don't remember when you started joining in with the rest of us, I suppose it happened gradually, but it didn't take too long. I do, however, remember your first entry in your writing book… you picked up your grey lead in your fist and scribbled all over your page. Do you know that your mum told me that you had hardly picked up a pencil before you started school? I wondered how I was going to teach you, I knew you were clever and full of life, but I didn't know how to break through to you.

In term two we started an integrated unit on farming. You all got a toy animal to choose and you had to make a shelter for them and discover what they liked to eat and drink. I wanted you to choose first, so you could have the animal you most wanted; I wanted to fan any spark of interest I could detect, however small. You chose a turkey to take home as your project, so that night I went shopping. I bought a stamp of a turkey with a snow dome on top and turkeys inside it, something to encourage you, I thought. Then one day you drew a picture of a turkey – it was amazing, I couldn't believe that this picture had come from someone who didn't even like to use pencils. Boy did I praise you over that; I was nearly moved to tears when I showed your mum. I was so proud of you.

By third term you were continually amazing me. You were reading above the class average and writing your own sentences. As I slipped writing samples into your file, I looked at the first entry in your writing book and then at what you were writing now. I showed the two pages around the office. 'Look at how far my Luke has come this year, isn't he amazing?' I think that anyone you meet in your life will have to admit that – yes, you are amazing.

In fourth term, a week or two before the end of term, I lost one of my cats in a terrible accident. On a Thursday night I was at the animal hospital most of the night and came to school only having had three hours sleep. Before school I had been crying again, but by the time the class started to arrive at school I had dried the tears and made myself look presentable.

It was a Friday, so you had art for the first hour and I was using the time before school to correct work. I was kneeling on the floor with books spread out around me. You walked in and came up to me and we were the same height. You put your hand on my back and rubbed it, you looked down into my face and said in the tenderest of voices, 'Are you all right? You look really tired.' Later that day I was still correcting books, you came up and stroked my back again and said, 'You look so beautiful today, just so beautiful.' You stroked the pale blue scarf in my hair and now I'll never forget what I was wearing that day. Throughout that day you cuddled my legs as I walked around the classroom. It made walking difficult, but I was glad to have you around.

As strange as it sounds, I feel like we have a bond. I guess it's like the bond between a mother and a child, but it's not quite that, maybe I'll know for myself one day.

At university, in one of our less useless subjects, we brainstormed the various roles of a teacher, things like: mediator, mentor, first aid administrator, secretary, wiper of tears, detective, finder of spare hats… bringing up the rear. In all these brainstorms was the role of educator. The academic aspect of teaching, can only fill so much of a year, the rest involves those human interactions, which we are not taught about at university. While learning about how to extend your 'zone of proximal development' did come in handy, it's children like you, Luke, who teach us the things we really need to know.

I often say to people, 'Teaching is such a weird job. What other profession is there where you are responsible (in so may ways) for the social, emotional and educational needs of so many people? You spend all day every day with them for a year, sometimes they drive you crazy, but then you learn to love them. Then all of a sudden they get taken away from you and it starts all over again.'

As I read over this letter to you, Luke, I realise that there are about 15 alternative letters that I could have written about children who have touched my life this year and helped me grow as a teacher. But you are the one who stands out the most; we have tested each other's boundaries and stretched each other's limits. A year later we are both better people for having shared each other's lives.

If I have the good fortune to touch the life of a child like you each year, I will consider myself a fortunate teacher. If you are the only child I will come across like this in my whole teaching career, it has already been worth it. We have taught each other this year and we have grown together. I consider myself to have been blessed to know you, Luke, and I hope that you will never forget me, because I will always remember you.

Your teacher,

Elizabeth

My global classroom

Peter D'Angelo

Empathy is one of a good teacher's best assets. Many bring it with them to the classroom and inculcate it in their students. Poet and teacher, Peter D'Angelo, who migrated to Australia as a child, takes us into his global classroom where empathy and language learning have always gone hand in hand. Peter teaches at Noble Park Secondary College, Victoria, Australia. He has had several books of poetry published.

Here Peter reflects on how perception, reflection and empathy affect his teaching and his students.

'My global classroom' was first published in EQ Australia, (Issue Four, Summer, 2000). It is reprinted here with permission.

I still vividly remember my first teaching day in 1979 when, fresh out of university and with fixed ideas on education, I found myself face to face with newly arrived Vietnamese and Cambodian refugee students sitting stone silent in a rundown classroom of the Noble Park Language Centre, near Melbourne.

It was my brief to teach them intensive English for six months, after which they would move on to regular schooling, to be replaced by another group who would then receive the same course.

It all sounded straightforward and achievable but, as I discovered ten minutes into the lesson, a degree proudly hanging on a study wall was no guarantee that, as a result of the process of teaching, learning was automatically going to occur.

FIRST LESSON

I began somewhat shakily with the standard introduction: 'Good morning class. My name is Mr D'Angelo and I will be your new English teacher this semester. I hope that we will have a very positive and productive time together.'

I waited expectantly for the usual student outburst, but nothing came – just an eerie silence of a kind that I have never encountered in any of the boisterous classrooms that had been part of my teaching rounds.

Once again I tried, hoping at least for a few mumbled voices. But, as before, nothing came. There was no hint from any of them that this was a classroom and I was their teacher and it was normal for them to put me through a 'baptism of fire'.

For one petrifying moment I felt completely lost, my mind scrambling back through all the lectures and tutorials hoping to find something that I could grab hold of in order to break this surreal deadlock.

Instinctively, I turned away from the group towards the blackboard and began to slowly print my name in large capital letters. Turning back to the class, I pointed at myself and said desperately, 'My name is Mr D'Angelo. MR D'ANGELO.'

But it was still the same unnerving silence and the vacant stare of expressionless eyes which seemed to be lost somewhere else in time. Feeling light-headed and as though I might collapse at any minute, I turned back to the board and printed my first name, hoping that its two syllables would be easier for the students to pronounce. 'Mr Peter. I am Mr Peter.'

I could feel the sweat trickling down my spine. Then it came, the first sound of a trembling voice from a boy sitting in the front row. 'M…Mita Pita.' He tried again. 'Mita Pita.'

'Yes, that's right. Yes, I am Mister Peter. Who are you?' I was pleading for a reply.

Slowly he looked up and I could see him desperately trying to form the words. 'You Trung,' he said. 'You Trung,' he repeated, gaining confidence.

'Yes, that's right!' I almost screamed because, finally, I had broken through the wall of silence and it didn't matter that the pronoun was wrong. Communication had just begun and I could hardly hide my joy. 'Yes, you are Trung and I am Mister Peter. Hello Trung, how are you today?'

In the excitement, the others quickly sensed that something was going on and soon they were all telling me their names, which I feverishly wrote on the board.

This in itself was a learning experiences as it was my first contact with the exotic sounds of Sokha Sun, Nguyen Thi Tuyet, Phuoc My Lan and, of course, Huyn Duc Trung. I was having as much difficulty pronouncing their names as they originally had pronouncing mine and I quickly realised something that had been unheard of in teachers' college – in this class, education was going to be an interactive journey involving everyone.

TRUNG'S STORY

And so, we continued as we had started, day after day, week after week, my students soaking up the new language at an astonishing rate and me becoming more and more aware of their backgrounds and situations as their English proficiency increased.

Often we would gather around the tattered map of the world whose borders seemed to be changing daily and talk about how it felt to leave behind your country of birth and to start life again in a strange new land.

These conversations, although often tinged with sadness and longing, always had a certain spark of hope. It was this positive element that I would focus on to get my students to write about themselves and it was during one of these sessions that Trung quietly left his chair and walked up to my desk.

'Mita Pita. I want to tell you something Vietnam. I want to tell you saddest day of my life.'

He went on to detail how he, his mother and three younger sisters were forced to leave the family home under cover of darkness and how they walked for three days and nights through jungle to board an overcrowded fishing boat in the hope it would take them to Australia.

'We sleep on top each other, eat nothing five days. One night the pirate come and take six girl, kill two men. Lucky not my sister. Father can do nothing, gun at head. Mother scream and cry but nobody can fight the pirate.'

Trung stopped talking for a while, then looked at me again. 'Mita Pita, my English still not good, but you teach and help me a lot. You help me for my future, so I tell you this.'

I sat there in silence, humbled by his experience. I'd read accounts of people escaping war and persecution but to hear it so honestly first hand was to have a lasting effect on both my teaching career and my life.

... AND OTHER LESSONS

Inevitably, the time came for this first class of mine to move on. I remember sitting alone in my classroom on the last day of term, sifting through the stories and poems that the students had given me as souvenirs. I knew that I had been a part of something special and, as it turned out, it proved to be something that I would experience over and over again.

In the 1980s, my class was home to Poles, Afghans, Romanians, Turks, Russians, Armenians, El Salvadorians, Chileans, Peruvians, Mauritians, Samoans and Chinese. They were followed in the 90s by students from the former Yugoslavia, East Timorese, Eritreans, Somalians, Iraqis, Iranians, Palestinians and a host of other displaced and often traumatised students.

Sometimes their accounts of personal tragedy were so overwhelming that I began to question every value and belief I held. Yet, every time I was in danger of 'losing the plot', my students' reaffirmation of hope for themselves, their families and the future renewed my commitment to them and their education.

In the mid-1990s, I moved from the language centre to Noble Park Secondary College, a school that had taken many of my ex-pupils over the years. The move was fuelled by a series of organisational changes over time to the language centre and to education policy, which had left me disillusioned. I knew that it was time to move on and re-establish myself professionally and spiritually.

REUNION

The change proved to be just what I needed and teaching my former students once again proved as rewarding as it had the first time. They were still as eager and polite as they'd been in those early days and by the end of the first year in my new position, I'd become totally recharged professionally, especially knowing that I had reconnected with these students at another critical stage of their lives.

I have now been at the school for five years, during which time I have seen many students move on to tertiary education and the next stages of their lives.

Often they come back to visit and inevitably the conversation turns to those first weeks at the language centre. As always, I'm reminded of just how privileged I am to have been a part of their new lives in Australia.

I am also reminded of my own experience of migration when I was five years old, suddenly finding myself on a ship leaving Italy, crying and waving goodbye to my grandfather and not understanding why we were being separated.

On my first day at school in Australia, there was the strange sound of a language I had never heard before. I felt completely isolated and afraid as the other kids in the class sneered, using words that were meaningless to my ears yet were still able to make me shrivel to nothing inside.

It wasn't long before the teacher took me aside and, in a calm voice, began slowly to teach me the alphabet. In what seemed a very short time, the sounds around me became words, then sentences and stories, and soon I was able to understand and make sense of my new world.

This was the gift my first teacher gave to me. It is a gift I have always tried to give back to my students, hoping to revive in them the same sense of dignity and worth instilled in me so long ago.

I sometimes go back to the empty spot where the language centre once stood (it was physically moved to another site) and as I walk around, the past comes flooding back. Every feature of this area has its own special significance – its own memory and meaning – because it was here that I really came to understand that no matter what we've been through, we can all come together and begin to live in peace with ourselves, each other and the changing world.

I have learnt this from all of my students over 20 years. It has forged within me an unshakeable belief that, in essence, we are one family, united on common ground, no matter how far apart we might once have been.

2

Understanding Challenging Children and Children with Emotional and Behavioural Disorder

Understanding emotional and behavioural disorders in mainstream schools

Bill Rogers

All the teachers writing in this book have realised, early in their careers, that there are many factors in a child's life that affect their behaviour at school; we have little control over those factors:

▶ *disturbing patterns of family dysfunction*
▶ *disruptive parenting patterns*
▶ *substance abuse*
▶ *structural poverty*
▶ *long-term unemployment*
▶ *significant lack of positive male role-modelling in male children*
▶ *characteristic diet of the child*
▶ *the role, extent and kind of TV characteristically watched by the child.*

(Howell, 1993; Rutter et al, 1979; Rogers, 1994, 2003a)

Even factors such as how race, ethnicity and gender are typically communicated in family dynamics can affect behaviour in self-defeating ways in a community like a school.

What all these teachers have done is to 'devictimise' the child not 'revictimise' him in the school setting. While many of the factors – noted above – can significantly affect a child's behaviour and self-perception (self-concept and self-esteem), they do not automatically bind him to dysfunctional self-coping, poor peer relationships and failure.

These teachers – unfailingly – enable these children to believe in themselves and to value learning. They also encourage the child to find a positive sense of peer acceptance.

Even if a child is 'at risk' (from family circumstances, special needs considerations or poor or dysfunctional behaviour at school) it is likely that they will be attending school on a more or less regular basis – particularly so at primary level. It is here, at school, that teachers (supporting each other) can make a difference. Children spend a third of their waking day at school. School can, and does, awaken a child's potential to *learn*; not just to learn literacy and numeracy skills (crucial as they are) but to learn that life has many possibilities – and that better, more positive, choices can be made in life. A third of their waking day in a school – that's a hefty (legally required) slice of their life and development. Most children enjoy school, and cope well with the formal and informal demands of schooling and education. That small percentage of children who are frequently challenging, or emotionally behaviourally disordered, need some extra level (and kind) of support.

Every teacher (one hopes) considers the special needs that some children have in areas of literacy and numeracy. Schools allocate teaching personnel and time for such students. Programmes are developed, plans are made and implemented. The teachers in this book apply the same sense of 'need' to children with behaviour concerns and behaviour disorders. These children, too, need support as well as necessary and appropriate discipline. This support will need to include a teaching component related to the students' 'academic' and 'social-survival skills' (Rogers, 2003a).

Schools are a *crucial* factor in the total social mix. As Elizabeth McPherson notes in her essay, at infant level the teacher may be, for some children, the most secure person in their day-to-day lives. In understanding EBD we need to understand that we work with, we relate to, a child – a person – not merely a difficult or challenging student.

▶ These essays affirm how teachers perceive challenging behaviour in their students. They note frankly how they sought *to understand* the disruptive and even bizarre behaviours exhibited by this (thankfully) small percentage of 'their children'.

▶ These teachers do not 'revictimise' a child because of where they are from, or their unfortunate progeny. They find ways to connect and then support.

▶ Communication – these teachers seek to gain a *common* bridge between child and teacher; no mean feat. They share how they found ways to connect.

▶ Each of these teachers honestly acknowledges the struggle, the frustrations, that working with challenging behaviour can occasion. They also *reflect on*, and learn from, that struggle.

▶ They acknowledge – and value greatly – the support of their colleagues in meeting the challenge of working with these children.

▶ 'Separating behaviour from the person' is difficult when a child's behaviour is lazy, rude, arrogant, mean-spirited, selfish, hostile and aggressive. While on the one hand these teachers advocate appropriate discipline (and consequences for disruptive or wrong behaviour) they do not hold grudges; they repair, rebuild and move on with the child. The teachers work with the child within their presence.

► They provide supportive 'structures', 'programmes' or 'plans' to teach the child the *behaviour skills* they need, particularly the skills they will need at school.

At the end of the day, however, it is not the programmes we provide (essential as they are to a child's learning) it is *the kind of teacher* who uses whatever teaching practice, strategy and content that makes the positive connections in these children's lives.

Measurement *of difference or* meaning *(when working with challenging children)*

Ken Sell

Ken is an experienced teacher of over 15 years. For the last three years he has been working as an Advisory Support Teacher for Education Queensland in the Nambour District on the Sunshine Coast. He has designed and implemented many in-service workshops relevant to primary and secondary teachers as well as advising administrators in areas of social equity and the interpersonal dynamics found within schools. Ken is presently finishing a research project relating to his work in schools. In this account Ken weaves the threads of three stories about children, which span over 15 years. These stories illustrate how, as teachers, we often significantly impact on the lives of our students. They illustrate how teachers demonstrate care and compassion through their role as a teacher. It is difficult, if not impossible, to 'measure' (with any accuracy) the effect of these many interactions we engage in as teachers. The meaning, however, can be demonstrated in the telling of the stories.

'He's dead.'
'How?'
'Car accident.'
'Is his father OK?'
'Yes, he wasn't in the car. He was running away.'

The look in the eyes suggested not all was right. Those around knew little of Michael, perhaps cared little for Michael. What could I do? I'm a teacher not a social worker. I'm not trained for this. Michael needed something, someone to connect with, to trust, to love. These were subjects not taught at university.

He was 11 when he died, hitch-hiking. Metal, blood, screams, silence.

Even in death when a cold calmness surrounds the noises of sirens and the living, there is time for onlookers to make assumptions. Families torn apart in seconds. The mother, the father, the brothers and sisters – how do they feel? The officer by the roadside can see his own family. Visions of faces smiling, angry, laughing, talking, playing, working, sleeping. How this would tear his family apart?

Michael's family was torn apart well before the crunching metal took hold.

His mother had left him; gone to the big city, problems in the mind. She ran.

His father was running but going nowhere. He ran to the pub.

Now it was Michael's turn to run. He ran head on.

What was he thinking as he stood by the roadside, finger out, rain dripping, waiting for a stranger to become his friend, to drive him away? He was 11 years old. What was he running from?

Michael had started the marathon long ago. Long before I'd met him. He'd been hurt, emptied of trust. Lost. His smile gave a different impression. One of hope – there's a chance; I'm not a bad kid. The smile hid the confusion. He was confused and so was I. His smile carried all the emotion attached to someone crying for love, his face looked for peace, but his body was angry. He couldn't connect, he didn't know how. His eyes were saying, 'Please look after me', but his voice was saying 'Get f___ed. You can't make me do it! What's happening? I don't want to go home. Can I go with you? It isn't my fault. Don't get too close to me. Shit I need help. Will you help?'

He's dead.

He can't be, he's only 11. A child, 11 years old, leaving home, in a stranger's car about to collide on the highway. Met head on by the loneliness of life, the noise of silence, the loneliness of death.

Did his father weep or was he too pissed? Did his mother weep? She may have – but for the overdose. People went to the funeral. It was a long time ago now. He'd be 26 all going well. Now I wonder who remembers the boy of 11.

Clinging to the cliffs, through the tunnels as black as the stockpiled coal on the sidings, the train made its way down the coast. Like that night of death, there was a coldness about the air from the south as it shot up the escarpment. I was leaving one kind of work behind, apprehensive as to what to expect as the train pulled into the platform that is a university.

I know I could not have stopped Michael's death, but my training as a teacher left me ill-equipped to recognise the problems with Michael, to cope with Michael's emotional disturbances or to teach Michael about himself. The years of further education in an institution that pays scant attention to social justice in terms other than theoretical was never going to prepare me for Michael.

Like the officer at the roadside I made assumptions. I thought those at the cutting edge would have an educated memory. It wasn't as I thought.

When I walked into the university I was clear in my thoughts about education. I had vision, compassion and intent. When I walked out a qualified teacher I suffered from fragmentation of thought and mixed messages about pedagogy, unable to declare with any confidence what education is all about.

Teaching, like parenting, doesn't come with a ready-made formula. Both Michael's parents and I made many mistakes. I'm lucky enough to have been able to learn from mine. I cried for Michael but I didn't know why.

Much later I found out.

GEE, YOU'RE A GOOD BLOKE!

Years later my aunt told me that regardless of what's happened, *leaving the door open* is the most important thing when working with people.

But sometimes finding the spare key to my house is difficult enough, let alone the key to the minds of students so they realise they have unconditional access into our classroom. Even though sometimes when I do find the 'key' and open the door some students won't come in this doesn't mean we should be selective in our invitations to enter; far from it. I firmly believe we do make a difference to the lives of all students we come in contact with.

It is the *type* of difference that is important.

This first story is a simple and uncomplicated one about the influence we have on children both young and adolescent. Recently on the ABC Radio National I heard someone talking about resilience. The point he was making is that although a group of children can grow up in very similar circumstances (namely structural poverty), some end up contributing positively to society while others are a cost to it. The man on the radio believes the difference is partly due to the *quality* rather than quantity of childcare given to the child that makes the difference.

Teacher *quantity* of care is easily 'measurable' by those outside the relationship. However, it is a far more difficult task to measure the quality of the care we give students because of the subjective nature of quality relationships and the fact that the results are not always immediate.

Listening to these ideas about resilience and the difference we as teachers make reminded me of the time I was given a nice bottle of red wine some five years after I had taught a child in Year 2. Unbeknown to me this child was miserable and hated Year 1, and he was finding it difficult to come to school each morning. When I was leaving the school the parent of this child gave me the bottle of wine in recognition of the work I had done in 'turning her son around' all those years ago.

'Thanks, but what did I do?' I asked the parent of a child heading down the path of school refusal.

She told me that she remembered the day her son came home and said now he liked going to school. When she asked him why, he said, 'Mr Sell said, "Gee, you're a good bloke".'

Five words of encouragement to the boy. At the time I thought nothing of it. However, five years later I was told of it and nearly a further five years later I began to understand what quality really is. So now when the economic rationalists come to measure my performance I say to them – when they look miserable and don't really want to be at work – 'Gee, you're a good bloke'.

TERRY

Like the first story this one is also about a boy who lived in structural poverty and despair. The previous year Terry nearly succeeded in providing a very well-organised and experienced Year 1 teacher with an opportunity to have a 'nervous breakdown'. She refused but did suffer a great deal in the meantime and was exhausted by the end of the year. I wasn't going to become his second victim.

But how could I prevent this from happening? I worked on two things. First I gathered as much information as possible about past teacher experiences and became determined to avoid those situations that lead to conflict. Not an easy task given Terry's need to be the boss of everything. Secondly, I decided that Terry needed a trusting relationship if he was to develop the social skills expected and this relationship would not be created through coercion. All that aside, I still had to deal with a boy whose life's picture was less than happy. After two weeks of bloody hard work I decided that this child needed only one rule to follow.

The rule was that *he was not to infringe on others' rights*.

Nothing else. Pretty simple.

What does it mean?

Good question and one I worked on throughout the year. In his language the rule became: *he has to get along with others*.

This meant he didn't have to do his school work, line up, sit on the carpet, join in group work or anything if he didn't want to; *however*, when he was interacting with others (which he really wanted to do) he simply had to get along with them. Of course to teach the boy the skills he needed to get along with others I needed help. This was a problem too big for me alone. Realising it was a shared problem I enlisted the other students in the class to help and help they did. Before we made our plans it was important to know what we were all talking about and what the problem was. As a group with a shared problem we informed each other by being quite transparent about the problem. We then mapped the boy's misbehaviour so we could all recognise it as it happened and then we had a plan to do something about it.

We agreed the problem was that: *usually when Terry doesn't get his own way he throws a tantrum*.

Then we used a very transparent mapping process which the whole class, with the student, helps to construct. It is a very interesting process and one I've since used repeatedly with varying degrees of success.

I wrote on the board:

1 Terry wants to be the Boss. (He replied, 'Do not', and rubbed it off the board.)
2 Terry becomes verbally aggressive. ('F___in' don't', as he rubbed it off the board.)
3 Terry becomes physically aggressive. ('Bullsh_t!' as he kicks the furniture around the room and rubs it off the board.)
4 I have to 'remove' Terry from the room. ('Can't do that. I know my rights', as he is 'removed' kicking and screaming.)
5 Terry in a calm manner wants to return after about five minutes (and he does).

All through this Terry 'did not want to know'. This was a very big room full of 'mirrors' for this student and I feel he didn't like what he saw. In his discussion he proceeded to rub out each part as I wrote it up. The next day I wrote the same thing on a piece of paper with a felt pen and this time he accepted it.

By doing this we gave Terry a very good idea about his own behaviour and how his peers saw his behaviour at times. It also provided an 'instrument' for me – as his teacher – and the other students to identify what was coming next. It was great to watch them say to Terry, 'You're up to number 2. Do you really want to do this?'

Of course there was far more to it than I've described. But we were confronting the reality as we saw it and we found agreement to that reality and the belief that it could move forward in a learning context rather than one of mere containment or management.

I firmly believe that if we put behaviour in the context of education we can look at new and creative ways of developing teaching practice based on learning theory. With Terry we spent a lot of time giving him an opportunity to recognise his current inappropriate behaviour and then learn the skills to change the mis-behaviour. We had an open door policy for Terry, despite his misbehaviours, and we helped him change the picture in his own mind of schools and people in authority. His peers rallied to the cause like neighbours can rally together when faced with disaster that could destroy their community. They, too, learnt new skills about dealing with difficult people.

Before he left, just prior to the end of the year, he was still occasionally telling someone where to go, doing next to no school work set by me (he was already very good at readin', writing and the other thing) and generally misbehaving. I asked him what he had learnt in Year 2 at this school.

He replied, 'Mr Sell, I've learned to get on with people.'

Try measuring that.

Changing perceptions of challenging behaviour: Tom and his teacher

Larry Taylor

Larry was transferred to a new and rapidly growing school a few weeks before the end of term three and given a 2/4 class. The children were drawn from eight different classes. The school was growing so fast that the classroom was a temporarily partitioned off section of the school library which had been partitioned once already and currently was home to a Year 6 class.

The children, without exception, were feeling unwanted and uncared for, having been uprooted from their existing classes so far into the year. They were less than impressed by their 'new' home and more than a little unsure of their 'new' teacher. He had to deals with tears and anger as he helped them move, and cope with the angst from parents as well.

Larry shares the 'strategies' that connected with his challenging students, noting that there are no 'formulas' for building the sorts of relationships that encourage positive change in a child's perception and behaviour.

One of this group was a Year 4 boy named Tom. Unhappy with his new lot, he dealt with this situation with an approach that some might call 'creative disobedience'. When the group lined up after breaks, Tom would be in the vicinity of the line leaning against a post. When asked to join the line properly, he would do so but stretch out his hand to the post and lean slightly towards it. When the line moved he would wait until the last moment to release contact with the post. He looked at me at each stage with a look that dared me to say something. When I made the 'mistake' of doing so, the immediate response was along the lines of 'What? I'm in line'.

This type of scenario was also regularly played out in class. Tom would speak when silence was required, speak louder than necessary when quiet talk was asked for, be last to sit down when quickness was needed and so on. These actions, however, were always accompanied by a well thought out, if somewhat manufactured, 'good reason'. I'm sure all of this was Tom's way of letting me know that he was not happy about being moved from his previous class. Instead of simply telling him what he was doing was inappropriate, 'Tom, keep your voice down, thank you', I found asking a question, such as, 'Are you doing what everyone else is doing?' was the more effective strategy (because Tom always had a 'reasonable' answer).

There were several other students in the group posing problems of their own, as well as Tom, and I took every opportunity to build a relationship with them as well. I did this by asking questions to find out what they were interested in and what they did in their spare time. With Tom it was like pulling teeth initially; there was a great reluctance on his part to give me more than monosyllabic responses. As I showed more interest, however, he grudgingly gave more information. I made numerous attempts to hook into these interests, with little success, and I was becoming frustrated by the whole experience. The rest of the class were beginning to adjust to their new circumstances, but problems with Tom continued. I decided that whenever I needed to speak to Tom about some problem I would call him over and speak to him quietly one-on-one so that less attention was drawn to the problem, but Tom frequently countered this by loudly saying, 'I didn't do anything!', or something similar, as he approached me.

There were times when juggling razor sharp knives in busy traffic seemed a more attractive proposition than going to work. I spent many days and nights pondering how best to deal with this – and I should add that we had regular class meetings from day one, where we all talked about what we were thinking and feeling about the changes we had been subject to. We also did 'getting to know you' and team-building activities, mixed in with a healthy dose of fun, but Tom steadfastly refused to buy into any of this. Then one day, unexpectedly, in a matter of minutes, everything changed forever. I had not thought through the particular strategy that I ended up using. When the breakthrough came, it did so from a spur of the moment action on my part.

Without waiting for a problem to occur, I once again called Tom out to speak to me. My request was greeted by the now predictable loud voice, saying, 'What did I do now?', to which I quietly replied, 'You're not in trouble.' His demeanour changed instantly. I then sat on the carpet in front of a whiteboard divider and invited Tom to do the same. I picked up a whiteboard marker pen, drew a circle on the board and wrote Tom's name in it. I then said, 'This is what I know about you'. I drew a line out from the circle and at the end wrote 'likes' and then began saying and listing the things Tom had been telling me he liked. Then I drew a second line and at the end wrote 'friends' and then spoke and wrote down the friends he had talked about. I continued with 'good at', 'groups', 'music', 'TV shows', 'movies', 'books' and anything that I remembered that he had told me. I resisted the temptation to write anything that he might perceive as 'negative' and focused only on the 'positives'.

Tom mostly sat quietly and listened, occasionally correcting, clarifying or adding to some piece of information I was listing. I acknowledged these additions by amending what I had written and discussing some points with him. We were having a 'real' conversation for the first time and it was a pleasant experience. What happened next took me completely by surprise. Tom asked for the whiteboard marker, he then drew a circle on the board and wrote my name in it. He drew a line from the circle and then wrote 'likes' and began listing things like 'sketching' and 'computers'. As he went on listing things like 'good at science and maths', I became more and more amazed at how much he had learnt about me. But the last two things he wrote surprised me most of all. He wrote that I was 'friendly' and 'cared about kids'. If anyone had asked me how Tom perceived me, those two items would probably have been the last two things I would have ever considered. From that moment on Tom and I got on really well. There was a new-found respect that altered all our perceptions and interactions from that moment on. Tom left the school and the area at the end of the year. Two years later he returned to pay me a visit and the mutual respect was still there. I was interested in being updated on how he was going and what he was currently doing. He seemed to be equally interested in how I was going as I answered his similar questions about me.

When I look back on those early months with Tom, I think that the strategy I had spontaneously used allowed Tom to see that my overall perception of him was favourable. I had included words like 'friendly' too, because he was, towards everyone else. It also gave Tom some control, in that he was able to update or amend my perceptions of him as we went, something he would not normally have been able to do – at least, not usually in a positive way. Although I didn't think of the other half of this strategy, the half that Tom used, I now realise that I could have invited him to take the pen and list what he knew about me, having already modelled the process using him as the example. A possibly risky venture granted, but nevertheless informative. The value in doing so was, firstly, that Tom was now in control of the interaction, something he often tried to be anyway, although this was a different and more positive type of control. Secondly, it gave me an insight into how Tom perceived me. This was something that I often attempted to influence by my actions, but – prior to Tom's revelations – I had judged my actions to be unsuccessful and Tom's perception of me to be unfavourable. Obviously I could not have been more wrong. Clearly Tom had been unwilling to share anything favourable he had learnt about me, until after I had first shared – in an 'organised' way – the favourable impressions I had formed of him.

Finding a connection point for change in behaviour: Alex 'wins a race'

Karen Kearney

Karen shares her journey with a 12 year old and how she helped him to 'belong'.

A year six student (who we shall call Alex) had a one per cent attendance record and read at 'beginners' level. Alex had difficulty completing tasks and was assigned a peer tutor. When he did attend school, he spent a great deal of time with teachers from the Special Education Unit. Alex lacked social skills and behaved aggressively toward other students. Not surprisingly, he spent most of his lunch and recess time under administrative supervision.

In this short essay Karen shows how she was able to find a connection point for a change in the student's sense of belonging at school.

During the first lesson for which I took the class (as a student teacher) I attempted to establish a rapport with Alex, but he responded by covering his work and placing his head on the desk. Alex stated that he 'knew what to do' and that his peer tutor would help him if he had any problems. I subsequently actively observed Alex's activities and noted that half way through the lesson, he had not attempted the task.

Later, I discretely asked Alex why he had not started the activity and he replied that he was 'not interested'. In an effort to identify motivators that could be adapted to aid Alex's education I asked what did interest him and he replied 'running and sport'. I therefore suggested to Alex that if he finished his work I would take the class for a run in preparation for the upcoming athletics carnival.

Alex immediately commenced to put some effort into the task – although he did rush, was initially reluctant to accept assistance and demonstrated a short concentration span. During the next 20 minutes, Alex sought immediate progression to the sports activity by constantly claiming to have finished the task. On each occasion I acknowledged his efforts and encouraged him to continue. When Alex did eventually complete the task, his personal satisfaction was quite evident.

I adjourned the class to the oval soon afterwards. Alex was very enthusiastic and difficult to quieten. I informed the students that we would 'run the first lap as a slow jog to warm up' and then do some stretching. The race was to be then run with a requirement that runners stay within the marked lanes. As an incentive, I informed the students that anyone who obeyed the rules and completed the race before I did would receive a prize.

Alex and a few other children immediately raced around the oval during the warm-up lap. He then approached me and stated that he had won. I asked him what my instructions were for the first lap, but he did not reply. I restated my instructions and then commenced some stretching exercises. I asked Alex if he knew of any stretches; he did and *ably demonstrated an exercise to the class*. Alex's turn (possibly first ever) at peer tutoring appeared to help him over his earlier disappointment and he enthusiastically completed all the stretching exercises.

We then conducted the race and at the finish, Alex informed me that he had won and wanted his prize. However, Alex had not stayed in the 'lanes' and I advised him that he was disqualified from receiving the prize because he had not complied with the rules. Two boys who completed the race correctly were awarded prizes.

As we returned to class Alex told me that he knew he was the fastest and that next time he would win. I replied that if he completed his work tomorrow, we would go out and race again.

The next day Alex completed his work and won an important race.

Choosing to teach: choosing to make a difference

Elizabeth McPherson

'When I chose to be a teacher people said that it would be difficult, but I certainly didn't think it would be like this...'

Elizabeth scans the students in her class group of infants and reflects on the wide range of emotional and behavioural disorders present in a number of her students. Aware that many of the 'reasons' for such behaviour lie outside her control, she nonetheless asks how a teacher can still make a difference.

When I was completing my BA and about to start my Bachelor of teaching, that's when all of our friends began, in earnest, their full scale attempts to dissuade me from the profession of teaching. Surely, I thought, what could be a more honourable, rewarding and fulfilling career than teaching? One year down the track and now I see what some of them meant. In my first year of teaching, I have been exposed to more diseases than a third world tourist, had less sleep than an emergency room doctor and been exposed to more unusual, strange, even bizarre people than an American talk show host.

At university, the proverbial 'they' enjoyed using analogies such as 'a child is like a flower, that when nurtured, will blossom into a thing of beauty'. Within the first week of knowing my more challenging students I was tempted to use the analogy 'some children are like weeds that take over the garden'. In a perfect world and even on a good day in the classroom, the first analogy is true, yet easy to forget. This year I have often needed to remind myself that my children are flowers, not 'weeds'.

On teaching rounds I felt a connection with the children with whom I worked, I felt close to them. But in my first year on the job I would have to say that I have (on the most part) felt like a mother with post-natal depression; longing to feel a connection to her child, but often feeling frustration and resentment. I found the first few months of teaching frustrating and heart breaking at times. Most of my children came from dysfunctional, violent or underprivileged homes and my classroom, despite my best efforts, was not the educational 'utopia' that I had hoped it would be.

Then one day I heard a startling statistic at a professional development session: that children hear one hundred negative comments to every one piece of encouragement they receive. The next day I walked into my classroom determined to focus on the positives. As the year has progressed I have learnt to become closer to my children and have come to accept them for who, and what, they are. One of my achievements this year has been developing a close relationship with a particular child who used to hide under tables and refuse to come out. This particular child refused to join the rest of the class or do anything, was petrified of the playground, of specialist classes, of theme days or anything out of the ordinary. Just recently at the school concert, not only did he go out on the stage, but he even led his line on; I was so proud. He still climbs up onto my lap whenever he is in need of 'sanctuary', but he has certainly blossomed.

Another one of my 'flowers' is the child of parents with heroin addiction. He was so violent that the assistant principal asked him to remain indoors at play times so as not to jeopardise the safety of others. This child has had a lot of trouble sitting still or focusing on his learning tasks and is extremely impulsive. I have always said to my own mum and dad, 'In what other job do you see potential doctors, teachers, parents; the person who will cure cancer, car thieves, murderers, prime ministers?' I looked at this beautiful little boy and thought, 'What will become of you, what chance do you have, what horrors do you go home to at night?' I have worked hard *while he is with us at school* to help make this child feel important. He sometimes sits on my chair and chooses people who are 'sitting beautifully' to go and get their play lunch, he is now the one who tries to have the 'hardest working table'. At one level I see myself reflected in him. When he is playing, he pretends to be me, and I know I am doing a good job when I like what I see.

I went to the birthday party of one girl in my class as a surprise guest, organised by her parents. While I was there, I was amazed to see that I was the one they all came to for conflict resolution, encouragement, opinions... I discovered that teachers are never 'off duty'. After the party, I drove another one of my students and her mother home. On the way home she brought to my attention that we, the teachers, are the ones who spend the most time with their children. In *some* cases we know the children better than their parents and may be the only really stable and positive influence in their lives. This is perhaps the first thing that made me want to become a teacher.

Teaching is definitely not a job you go into for the fame and glory, you do it to make a difference.

These days there is an ever-increasing push towards globalisation. As a result there has been an increased push towards technology in the classroom in addition to the traditional three Rs. As teachers become ever more accountable for the performance of their students, the academic side of schooling is pushed to the forefront of classroom planning while childhoods may be at risk of being marginalised.

I, too, – at times – have been guilty of pushing my students too hard and have needed to remind myself that they are only five years old. Talking to one of my parent helpers, I commented on one of my student's writing, 'Can you remember writing like this at this age?' To which she replied, 'I can't even remember learning to write in grade prep' (infants). We are putting more and more weight on little shoulders and I, for one, think that we should allow space for 'developmental play' in our work programmes.

During the lead up to the school concert, I was reminded of the importance of play in the lives of my students. We were heading off to an unscheduled rehearsal when one of my boys began to show obvious signs of distress. 'What about free time?' he said. 'Why are they making us do our dance again, we know how to do it…' As I thought about getting him a paper bag to breathe into, I was reminded, yet again, of the desperate need for play in children's overall development. I recall seeing a child from my mother's school who developed 'environmental autism' from having no stimulation as an infant. From birth he was left to lie in his cot for hours on end and as he grew he was never allowed to play with paints, play-dough, puzzles … anything that 'messed up the house'. As a result he was placed in a special school when he turned five. Although I make no claim to be an expert on this topic, I do claim to be genuinely scared by this story.

Some of the highlights of this year – as a teacher – have been:

► The time Corey cut the tip of Luke's finger off, and – carrying a hysterical Luke – I found myself drenched in blood.
► The time Lachlan told the Italian teacher that he was going to 'rip her f___ing arms off' and the numerous occasions on which he threatened to 'burn the f___ing school down'. (He didn't – thankfully. Later he would come over to me, hold me and seek reassurance that 'I was going to stay, wasn't I? Don't leave, Elizabeth!' I didn't.)
► The period of several weeks in which Luke refused to come out from under the table.
► The candid revelation of Nick's mother that she was a heroin addict (that helped explain why Nick was often late and why she often forgot to pick him up at the end of the school day and …).
► Finding out that some of my students are confusingly related through various torrid 'affairs' of their parents.
► The day that Damien's auntie got him in a head lock and practically ripped his ear off during a sports lesson I was conducting.
► Having dirt thrown in my eyes, and being kicked, punched and sworn at by a student on yard duty.
► Another teacher finding one of the students soaked to the bone (rolling in a puddle) because, in her words, she had decided to 'fall' repeatedly into a puddle.
► Seeing nits for the first time and many, many times since.

Every recess or lunchtime, I wait for the inevitable knock on the door announcing that one of my children needs an ice pack because they have been punched or kicked or are covered in some new strain of violent rash. All I could say to the other teachers (with a wry smile) was that I didn't give birth to them – *but I am their teacher*.

We live in a society where some of our children present as 'damaged goods' in school. *It is not their fault.*

At the end of my first year of teaching, I am left with one thin, elusive but crucial strand of idealism: If I can make a difference in one child's life, if one child finds some self-worth in my class, if one child makes something of themselves, then I have done my job.

I am a teacher.

3

Teaching Children with Emotional and Behavioural Disorder

INTRODUCTION

Bill Rogers

This is the longest chapter in the book; it is devoted to several accounts of how teachers have developed individual support programmes and plans for children with emotional behavioural disorders.

As noted earlier (p 16), while home background, parenting styles, family dysfunction, structural poverty, etc. can significantly affect a child's behaviour at school, such 'causal pathology' is not inevitable or immutable. Behaviour, like 'intelligence', is not fixed.

Behaviour is learned as well as conditioned. If we accept that 'conditioning' leads to challenging behaviour, that behaviour has been learnt – even if the genesis of that learning is forgotten by the child.

This chapter addresses a common theme, noted by all the teachers, that notwithstanding any 'causal pathology' contributing to behaviour and predisposition, a child always has the potential for *un*-learning, and developing *new* learning – providing they have adequate on-going support.

Sound principles of learning underlie this assumption. Even where a child has a behaviour disorder such as attention deficit hyperactivity disorder (ADHD), teachers will emphasise academic and social survival skills when they work with the child within the schooling context. Children with Tourette's syndrome, and Asperger's syndrome, have very often benefited from the concepts and strategies noted here.

Where a child has 'learnt' poor, inadequate, inappropriate or dysfunctional patterns of behaviour, teachers work with the child to directly teach new, appropriate self-coping behaviours that will strengthen a positive sense of self and learning and relationships at school.

All children want to belong; it is a central, social, need (Erickson, 1970; Dreikurs et al, 1982 and Maslow, 1972). The children described in these accounts often seek to belong in attentional or power-seeking ways; adverse, or even self-destructive, patterns of attention and power-seeking.

These teachers do not easily get sidetracked by those factors – in the child's behaviour patterns – over which they have no control. They focus on what they can do, *at school*, while the child is with them.

When addressing patterns of distracting, disruptive or dysfunctional behaviour, they ask:

▶ How *frequent* is the calling-out; the 'clownish' behaviour; the butting in; the pushing in line; the inappropriate loudness; the task avoidance; the challenging or oppositional behaviour, etc.?

▶ How *durable* is such attentional or power-seeking behaviour? Is such behaviour more than 'bad-day syndrome'?

▶ How *generally* is such behaviour observed? Is such behaviour frequent and durable in the grade/subject class or is such behaviour frequent and durable across all teachers (and support staff) who work with this child?

▶ How *intensely* is such behaviour displayed? There's a big difference (in teacher tolerance) between calling out and *loud* calling out, between a six-year-old quietly rolling on the mat, and loud, kinaesthetic rolling, or wandering, pushing, shoving …

When any *pattern* of behaviour (as above) is observed, these teachers – with their colleagues – developed a *whole-school plan* to give some structural, educational support to the child to learn new patterns of behaviour (Rogers, 2003a).

One, two, three, four, out the door – or STOP
(Straight To the Office Please)

Bette Blance

The day starts out well. The trip to school is uneventful, even though the long trip each day from home to school some-times brings its own pressures. At least there is time to think about the class and Bert. His behaviour is getting worse and Bette has spent so much of her waking time think-ing about him lately. What is she going to do?

Bette shares how she – with her colleagues – helped Bert to develop his own plan for his own behaviour.

These thoughts are common, with many anxious teachers wondering what to do about those children who choose behaviours that do not help their learning and disrupt the learning of others. Very often, as these behaviours are recalled, they crowd out any thoughts about the rest of the class and their learning. This adds feelings of guilt to the feeling of inadequacy as a teacher.

Much has been written about how to work with these students and teachers continue to try to solve the problems with a variety of actions.

Out of sheer frustration and not knowing what else to do, teachers send the child to the office with a note. They vainly hope the child will be 'fixed up' and sent back to try again for another day. While it does still happen, teachers today are less likely to want the child to come back fearful and remorseful. Whatever the motive the teacher has in sending the child out of the classroom, some students spend an inordinate amount of time on 'the pathway' between the classroom and the office.

What messages does this convey to the student who is sent to the office by the teacher? What kind of thoughts do students have as they set off for yet another interaction with one of the administrators?

Is it thoughts of 'Yeah! I've won again.'
Or 'I couldn't do the work anyway. This school sucks!!!'
Or 'What will my parents say this time?'
Or 'I knew I was a rotten kid, I've done it again! Why can't I be like the others?'
Or 'It wasn't my fault, I'll get that Jason when I get back to class, it's all his fault.'
Or even 'I haven't taken my tablet this morning.'

Whatever the thinking that accompanies the student as they go to the office, as teachers we need to ask ourselves, 'Has what I have just done (sending the child to the office) brought us closer together or has it pushed us further apart?'

Dr William Glasser, in his book *The Quality School* (1992), has written extensively about a 'lead management' approach in the classroom. He proposes that teachers need to provide a warm and caring environment and encourage responsibility by teaching the students to become self-managing.

If we do send children to the office for a particular set of behaviours or because they have reached a certain 'level' on our school behaviour plan, are we then enhancing or damaging the relationship that we really need to establish and maintain with the child?

In his book called *Behaviour Recovery* (1994, revised 2003), Bill Rogers proposes an approach in which the child is not simply sent to the office but 'the office' comes to the classroom so that the teacher remains involved.

In 1999 as school administrator I used this process with the six Year 3 classes for which I had responsibility. I encouraged the teachers to become involved in a trial of the process that would enable them to put the process in action. I asked them to act sooner rather than later so that behaviours did not escalate, creating even greater concern.

My initial actions were to conduct professional development sessions with the teachers so that they could take over the process as outlined in *Behaviour Recovery*. I discussed the importance of maintaining involvement in helping the children to make better choices. They were the ones who could be with the child consistently to encourage him or her to stick to a plan. The whole process itself would enhance the relationship with the child.

During our professional development we discussed the process and agreed to follow these procedures:

1 The teacher and the student *clarify the behaviour* and discuss why it was inappropriate.
2 The teacher *mirrors* the inappropriate behaviour so that the student can see what it looks like. ('Mirroring' involves the teacher showing the student what it is – specifically – about his behaviour that is inappropriate/unacceptable/ wrong). All mirroring is always conducted one-to-one *away from any other students*. The teacher will always ask the student's 'permission' before 'mirroring' their typical distracting or disruptive behaviour. e.g. 'Do you mind if I …?' 'I'd like to show you what it looks like when you call out lots of times in class …' This 'display' of their behaviour is brief and the teacher will physically step away a pace, to indicate she is out of 'student role'. The 'mirroring' gives the student a more concrete reflection of their behaviour, as it were.
3 Together the teacher and the student *draw pictures*, using dark colours, to further acknowledge the target behaviour.
4 The discussion around the pictures drawn would be about the *impact of the behaviour* on the other children in the class.
5 The student *rehearses better behaviour choices* in a second role play.
6 The teacher and the child *identify strengths* that will help the child to keep to the plan.
7 The teacher *encourages* better choices of behaviour in the classroom and *facilitates the self-evaluation*.

We developed a planning sheet (see Figure 1) that would be used in the discussion with the child and all agreed to try the process.

What have I been doing that is stopping my learning?	What will I be doing to help my learning?

My plan is to do more of ... _____

_____

My plan is to do less of ... _____

_____

Student signature _____

Teacher signature _____

Parent signature _____

Figure 1

My role was to respond to a note from the teacher when I was to take over the class while the class teacher used the *Behaviour Recovery* process. I also designed a self-evaluation book (see Figure 2) to enable the child to monitor their own behaviour and to let me know periodically how the plan was going. This was set out with a page for each day.

Is this how I want to school to be?			
I made great choices all session	☐	☐	☐
I made more good choices	☐	☐	☐
I didn't make good choices but I can do better next session	☐	☐	☐
Is what I am doing helping or hurting?			

Figure 2

Following the professional development we were ready to begin. The first message arrived. Bert had continued to talk after several warnings while the teacher was teaching the class. The teacher would like to try *Behaviour Recovery*. I went to the classroom to find that the children were engrossed in their own work and so I was able to support the teacher as she implemented the process.

We became involved in a role play where Bert became 'the teacher'. His jaw dropped as his teacher acted out nudging and talking behind his hand to his friend. His amusement at his teacher and the deputy principal taking on the roles could not be contained. He laughed at our antics. Now some teachers would believe that managing students is a serious business and that laughter was inappropriate. We believe that learning and fun are closely linked. We also believe that memory is enhanced by the fun and enjoyment that was inherent in this process. Bert also tried some of the managing techniques that the teacher had used in her classroom. This gave her information about her own style of managing students.

Following the role plays, the teacher set aside some one-to-one time to work with the child to formulate a plan for change. The plan included the self-evaluation book, which was used each session and verified by the teacher. A small notebook with a 'thumbs-up' sign on the front (found in most supermarkets) is the ideal size. A copy of the self-evaluation tool in Figure 2 was pasted on several pages of this notebook.

Bert was given control of how long he wanted to use the self-evaluation book. Inside the cover I had written the following information:

> *When you think that you no longer need this book and you can manage your own behaviour, please bring it to Mrs Blance for a surprise.*

After about three weeks, when Bert brought the book back to me, he stated that he would no longer need the book, as he was now 'self-managing'. I asked if he would like a certificate or to play a game. Surprise, surprise, he chose a game. We proceeded to the courtyard outside the office and with some string I tied a balloon to my leg. His task was to try to pop the balloon and mine was to try to keep the balloon out of his way (without running away). There was great hilarity as he tried to stand on the balloon. Thankfully he was able to do it before I ran out of steam.

To heighten the experience, and add to Bert's need for power and fun, I asked Bert if he would like to teach the game to his class. We went back to the classroom, where I asked the class about how Bert had been choosing to behave in class lately. They affirmed that he was now making much better behaviour choices. Bert then invited the class outside. He had the children line up, giving half the class a balloon to tie onto one foot with the other half of the class the task of popping it. In this way Bert was able to receive full recognition for the changes he had made in the way he was choosing to behave. The teacher reported on-going improvements in his behaviour.

The *Behaviour Recovery* process enables the teacher to maintain their contact and be fully involved in the *recovery* from the behaviours that hinder learning. Some teachers think that children need to be sorry for their behaviour. They think that by choosing language that implies guilt, the child will change. These behaviours are destructive to the relationship between the child and the teacher. If a child is laughing and looking forward to putting the plan into action or making better choices, they are working from a position of strength rather than a position of weakness.

The position of weakness may result from a number of responses. Children may choose the fight or flight response. They may back-chat or argue or they may withdraw. They may blame others and the self-talk adds to their feeling of inadequacy. If we want to work from a position of strength, *Behaviour Recovery* is an excellent process to use.

I did have some amusement from a note I received during my last days at that school, and while I was not involved in the process I often wondered how the role play went for this incident:

> *This student has been looking up rude words in the dictionary and showing his underwear to students who were lining up for school.*

There is always a way back: an individual behaviour management plan

Mara Smart, Mariette West and Pamela Curtain

Nick, a grade 6 student, was frequently in trouble for distracting and disruptive behaviour; frequent loud noises; touching and hitting others' belongings; task refusal; at times throwing things around the room; non-compliant behaviour. His behaviour was also creating peer-alienation.

Mara, Mariette and Pamela share how 'negotiated boundaries' and a consistent plan helped Nick change his attitude and behaviour and improve peer-acceptance.

Most schools have a downward vertical model for their school behaviour management plan. While school communities might discuss choice and negotiation, most expect students to conform to guidelines that begin with a warning and end with exclusion. Students then choose to behave or not to behave in the appropriate manner. If they continuously opt for the latter they can convince themselves that they're 'bad' and accept the downward spiral. Students can feel disempowered with no control and think it is futile to change their behaviour. In this paper we propose an alternative approach and present a case study of a student where this approach is working effectively.

'There is always a way back' (see Appendix, page 121) encourages school communities to revisualise the behaviour management structure as circular rather than vertical. This model encourages the student to think about where they are, where they would like to be and how they can get what they want. The plan is negotiated by the teacher, the deputy principal, the student and the parent, who all sign an agreement. The student draws a line from each marker back to the start and discusses ways to repair and rebuild relationships with their teacher and the class. The teacher is provided with a scripted plan to enable them to remain calm   and consistent when informing the student about their choices and consequences. When the teacher calmly places negotiated boundaries around the student, the student feels 'safe' – negative emotion is minimised, escalation is avoided and successful outcomes are facilitated. This is illustrated in the student's comment below:

I'm on marker one, I've made a mistake but I know there is always a way back. If I follow my plan and I make the right choices I can get back where I want to be. Even if I'm on marker two or marker three or marker four there's always a way back. The teachers want to help me, it's up to me to

*find my way back just like when I drew the lines from each marker back
to where I want to be on my plan.*

(See plan in Appendix)

Proactive relationship-building strategies are articulated in the plan; this is essential. Connections are made and sustained between the student and key players in the school. The adults are encouraged to ask themselves regularly if what they are about to do will bring them closer to the student or push them further apart. Ways to acknowledge the student's achievement of his goals that are student-valued, immediate, frequent and regular are also negotiated. Parental support is gained so that significant family members (like Nick's grandmother) are included.

Whole school support is organised so that the teacher is sustained by their colleagues. In the case of Nick (see Appendix) a behaviour management plan has been developed to incorporate a sense of supportive community and positive relationship building. Each morning Nick makes breakfast for himself and the deputy principal, and therefore appreciates the administrator's open door policy as a comfort zone and a place to settle down before the day. He is able to ring his grandmother when he needs the connection with family for added reassurance. A team case conference early in the year involved Nick's mother, his previous class and current class teachers, the senior guidance officer, a behaviour management support colleague, the principal and deputy principal and the support teacher for learning difficulties. A specific plan was developed to include roles and strategies as mentioned above and within the classroom and whole school community as indicated here:

Deputy principal:
▶ mentoring and open door policy
▶ co-developing individual behaviour management plan and modified programme with class teacher and trialling and modifying them (collaboratively)
▶ responding immediately to teacher's phone calls
▶ facilitating whole class exit from room when necessary and staying in empty room with student until he is calm again
▶ organising for the school counsellor/chaplain, a male mentor for Nick, to train in Freerk Ykema's 'Rock and Water' programme and lead the students through it. (This is a self-esteem development programme for students.)

Support teacher for learning difficulties and guidance officer:
▶ liaising with team so that Nick's academic needs are determined and provided for.

Mariette, Nick's class teacher, speaks of her experiences:

*My name is Mariette West. I teach Year 6/7 at Musgrave Hill State School
where we have a school-wide behaviour management plan. Before coming
to Australia I taught in a school in Canada for one year. Recently, however, it became obvious that the behaviour strategies I had used in the past*

don't work for all students and in particular not with one of the students in my class.

I was asked, a week into the new year, if I would take into my class a student who wasn't functioning in his previous class. The combination of students in his previous class was such that with Nick in the room as well, very little learning was happening for anyone in the room.

Nick's arrival into the classroom wasn't welcomed by those students who had been his classmates in the previous year. Nick's negative, attention-seeking behaviours became evident very quickly and these included:

▶ *making continuous loud noises*

▶ *hitting and touching others' belongings as he went past their desks*

▶ *refusing to complete any work*

▶ *throwing things around the room.*

After a month of trial and error dealing with Nick's behaviour, it became clear that I had to put into place a programme that was suited specifically to him. I begged for help. After meetings with his mother, previous teachers, the school psychologist who had worked with him in the past, and the administration team at our school we began to get an idea of where we had to go with Nick.

As a result of the meetings, Mara Smart and I began developing an individual behaviour management plan*. Nick was given four goals to focus on (e.g. work quietly, use computer only when allowed, hands and feet to himself and follow teacher's instructions). Each time Nick achieves a goal he is acknowledged. If he doesn't, then I have a specific four marker plan to follow.*

I have been following the plan for a week and a half. Nick seems to like the structure and most times does the right thing, but when he doesn't I know the steps to take. It takes the guess work out of it. I am optimistic that Nick will show improvement as long as I consistently follow the plan.

In discussing behaviour management the idea of a long, torturous visit to the dentist comes to mind. The prying, poking and prodding is like the intervention we put in place for some students and their families, who sometimes see us as interfering 'do-gooders'. It hurts. It touches nerves. It gets too close. The intervention places stresses and pressures on everybody in the student's 'system'. Often the situation seems to worsen before it improves. We have witnessed the pain of parents coming to grips with the consequences of their child's aggressive and, sometimes violent, interactions with fellow students and staff. Often they inflict their anger on those intervening. Like dentists, perhaps, we need to hang in there for as long as it takes; to build trust, to send calm, positive messages to ourselves and everyone involved, to reassure and to keep them all informed so they know in advance that some things will work and others might not.

In their book *The School for Quality Learning*, Crawford, Bodine and Hoglund write that all individuals are driven by genetically transmitted needs that serve as instructions for attempting to live their lives. They are the need to *survive*, the need to *belong*, the need to gain *personal power*, the need to have *fun* and the need to be *free*. Influenced by past experiences everyone adds to their needs differently. We all have our own memories of need-satisfying behaviours specific to our own unique life experiences. These pleasurable memories make up our *quality world* and become the most important part of our life. For most of us, this quality world is composed of pictures (or perceptions) representing what we enjoy in life. These perceptions become the standard for behavioural choices. When what is happening in our lives matches our *quality world pictures* we feel in control. When what is happening in our lives does not match our quality world pictures the mismatch is often a source of stress.

We all have a quality world picture of the teacher we want to be, of the classroom environment we want to develop. We all have a quality world picture of what we want our students to be like. We make behavioural choices to match our pictures. When we think, feel or act in a way that does not match our picture of the teacher we want to be, or when children act in a way that does not match our picture of the students we want to teach, we can choose frustration and anger.

When a school and its teachers are in the quality world of students they are more likely to make behavioural choices that can help them get what they need. Individual behaviour management plans can help us restructure students' school days so that school is part of their quality world.

At Musgrave Hill State School we believe that 'there is always a way back' for our students. We intervene with team case conferences, individual behaviour management plans and modified weekly programmes which all involve a wide range of people in the student's system. The modified programme means that Nick's day is varied so that his 'multiple intelligences' are harnessed, his basic needs can be added to and the responsibility for teaching him is collegially shared across several staff members (see Appendix).

Extensive collegial support structures underpin all our strategies. These structures include, time-out partners across the school, appropriate behaviour classroom at break times, a behaviour management teacher onsite, a male chaplain/counsellor, a formal mentoring programme with mentors trained by Griffith University (Gold Coast) and an Establishing Teachers Network which is co-ordinated by four Musgrave Hill teachers across the local area. Students at risk are a whole school shared challenge and with this supportive environment, individual weekly programmes can help shift the school into their 'quality world'. Students can then recognise that survival, belonging, personal power, freedom and fun are accessible and that with effort and understanding from all concerned 'there is always a way back'.

Helping a child change his behaviour and his short attention span

Kerrie Miller

Kerrie works with young children with special needs in learning and behaviour. She shares an account of how a behaviour recovery plan helped a young student refocus his attention and learning in class. This plan helped change the focus from discipline and correction to learning support.

I work with a wonderful young man called Matt who has Downs syndrome. He has a very short concentration span and was constantly interrupting the class learning time by rolling on the floor and playing with his shoelaces. Constant verbal reminding was not working for him in fact it was actually contributing to the class disruption – it was affecting other students' attention and learning.

Based on the *Behaviour Recovery* model (Rogers, 1994 revised 2003) I decided to try picture cues to help in our behavioural modification task. I drew Matt rolling on the floor and emphasised the sad faces of his friends and teacher. (On discussion, Matt didn't like the picture.) I also drew another picture (some simple 'stick figure' drawings) – Matt sitting up and listening intently. The faces of his peers were happy and his teacher's face was relaxed and happy. (Matt loved this picture and wanted to show everyone.) These pictures (the picture cues) became Matt's personal behaviour plan. These pictures were used in the one-to-one behaviour-teaching sessions as a basis for *clear* awareness of required behaviour and as a basis for discussion and *behaviour* rehearsal.

In class time the picture cues became his reminder cards; I used them to remind and encourage Matt. Initially during classroom time, particularly during whole-class teaching time when the students sit on the carpet at the front of the room, I would draw Matt's attention to the cards and he would correct his behaviour immediately. I gradually reduced my interaction – to tapping the card and non-verbal contribution – until all I had to do was use Makaton cues (sign-language) to direct his attention to the cards.

The overall result of this programme was that Matt's behaviour improved rapidly, as did the behaviour of the rest of the class (this was an unintentioned bonus!). The non-verbal instruction (and reminder cues) allowed the learning time for the whole class not to be interrupted.

I now use picture cues, as part of my behaviour support, to modify specific behaviours of other students and have had great success.

AD/HD *and teaching academic survival behaviours*

Bill Rogers

A number of the children who present with emotional behavioural disorder have been diagnosed with AD/HD – attention deficit/hyperactivity disorder. Further many of these children take medication for this 'disorder' such as Ritalin or Dexamphetamine (both amphetamine by-products, 'stimulants' that can assist concentration and attentiveness).

When an older student says, 'I can't help what I do because I've got ADD' we respond with a supportive wink, 'Well we'll have to teach you then'.

My colleagues and I are not unsympathetic to behaviour disorders such as AD/HD, or autistic spectrum behaviour such as Asperger's syndrome; we have learned that children with special needs and behaviour disorders have a genuine learning need (see O'Brien, 1990; Rogers, 2003; Cooper, 1997b). This knowledge is – at times – held in creative tension with the stress of working with children with EBD. In mainstream schools the degree and extent of support is not always available for the development of behaviour support programmes.

We are also aware that many children with behaviour disorders take prescribed medication for such behaviour disorders.[1] However, if a child is on medication they will still need some form of behaviour plan to assist them *while at school*. Medication can affect, significantly affect (at times), brain chemistry and aspects of physiological behaviour. Medication cannot – obviously – teach a child what to do with any increased concentration and attentiveness that might arise from prescription medication for AD/HD.

All the teachers who have shared their journey in this book have emphasised how they spent *time* with a child (with challenging behaviour or emotional behavioural disorder) teaching alternative patterns of behaviour.

For example, take an older child (with ADD) at primary or secondary level who finds it very difficult to get settled or focused during 'on-task' learning time: their desk is overly cluttered, they can't find the right book for that activity, they've got a pencil case that needs a crane to get it on the desk. In such cases many teachers now develop a personal plan for the student (developed out of class time). This plan focuses on deceptively basic 'academic survival skills' (Rogers, 2003a) and is centred in a supportive one-to-one programme emphasising positive role play, behaviour-rehearsal, cueing and feedback. The aim is always to increase the child's behaviour self-awareness and lead them to self-monitoring/regulating behaviour. In the example of increasing a student's on-task skill the plan focuses on:

▶ **Teaching** the student how to have an organised and uncluttered desk.

▶ **Colour-coding** books so they know – quickly – what book or what subject they need to have on their desk. Only *that* book on the table at *that* time.

▶ 'Garaging' the big pencil case (that crowds the desk and is a time/visual distractor) and having a much smaller, and accessible, **table pencil case** on the desk, with only a red and a blue pen (checked once a week for viability), pencil (no sharpener), ruler and eraser. Some students will spend several or more minutes playing with little toys – or other special paraphernalia – in that large pencil case. Often, too, they do not have a pen that actually works.

▶ Teaching the student through **one-to-one role play** how to: approach a learning task, asking themself questions such as '*What* am I asked to think about / do right now?' (whether 'board'/book/worksheet or group task) and then begin the task (bit by bit) with date, margin, etc. This is all practised with the student in one-to-one behaviour recovery sessions (Rogers, 2003a) (always away from the audience of his peers, normally in 'non-classroom' times).

▶ Each three to five minutes the class teacher will come to the child's table to **check** and to *briefly* **encourage** them in their plan. A small reminder card stays on the child's desk (if they want) as a visual *aide memoire* with the key reminder points of their plan.

▶ The message is clearly communicated (in the one-to-one sessions) that 'If you need teacher help this is *how* you get it …'. We never assume, always **explain clearly** *how* **to fairly gain teacher assistance**. This is to counteract easy calling out or 'wandering'. Even such behaviour as seeking teacher assistance can be practised.

The teacher will frequently encourage the child – during class work time – by giving brief, positive, quiet, private and *descriptive* feedback, e.g. 'You started quickly. You got your table pencil case out …' 'You've written half a page Craig … and you remembered to use all the words we brainwaved about … I notice you've added a few more of your own'.

ENCOURAGEMENT

As with all encouragement we avoid overly public encouragement in the sense of broadcasting to other students. At upper primary and secondary level students tend to be easily embarrassed by public encouragement (such as mentioning or showing an individual's work to the whole class – something we should never do without their permission). By 'private' encouragement I mean the quiet word (as we move around the room during on-task learning time): the quiet, often brief, descriptive aside or comment.

Some children with EBD do not respond positively to the sorts of glowing praise that teachers give, such as, 'That's great work Sean!' Some students will respond with, 'No it's not, it's rubbish!' Conversely some students may only believe a teacher is valuing them (and their work) if they are frequently praised in glowing terms such as 'brilliant', 'fantastic', 'marvellous', 'wonderful', 'great' … We are on safer, fairer, surer ground when we *describe* (rather than evaluate); avoiding non-specific words like 'fantastic' and 'brilliant'.

While not ignoring a student's mistakes or errors in their classwork (these can obviously be supportively acknowledged) it is not helpful to *disclaim*, or judgementally *qualify*, a student's effort in work or behaviour. Easy qualifiers such as 'Why?', 'But' and 'If only' will often mean the child focuses on the last part of the feedback, e.g: 'You've remembered many times, today, to put your hand up without calling out (the positive feedback for the behaviour plan) – *if only you would do that all the time we would have a much happier class, wouldn't we?*', 'You've done half a page of maths so far, *why can't you do that all the time?*', 'You've completed the exercises *but there are too many mistakes.*'

Teachers who give such qualified feedback I'm sure intend well. But I wonder how we (as adults) in a similar situation might feel and how such feelings might affect our on-going effort.

When addressing a student's errors (in 'academic' learning and in behaviour), our tone and manner are as important as our words. The simplest corrective is to acknowledge and affirm the student's effort and *supportively note the area for correction*, fine-tuning or changing. For example:

> *You have been very careful in using all the terms for sea mammals and how they breathe. I couldn't quite understand what this part here means … When you read it through you'll see what I mean. Check the spelling of porpoise.*
>
> *I'm glad you managed to answer all the topic questions – some of them were not so easy, were they? Well done! Remember to put the date on and the topic heading.*

Descriptive feedback (and encouragement) always takes a little longer but is more constructive than a grading (8 out of 10 or 'B') with a 'well done' or 'good effort'. These terms don't carry any information about *what* was 'well done' or 'good' about a student's work or behaviour.

Children with AD/HD do sometimes miscue and rush their work and they will need support to become thoughtful and paced learners. Behaviour plans noted in this and other essays give students a structure for that skill development.

A Tall Order: a challenging student on
day one and after

Patsy Finger

Patsy Finger describes the 'tall order' of balancing rights and responsibilities with 11 year olds. She shares how she developed an individual and whole-class focus for responsible student behaviour.

Patsy recalls her first day back at school after a relaxing, refreshing Christmas holiday. Enthusiastic and looking forward to the new year, she was feeling very positive. The Year 6 children were welcomed warmly to the classroom ...

FIRST ENCOUNTERS

Unexpectedly, a noisy young boy caught my attention as he reluctantly entered with a parent. As he approached he declared that he wasn't staying. In fact, he insisted that he was leaving. I was bewildered because he claimed to have no books or any other belongings to put into his desk. He had 'rights', he blasted at me and stubbornly refused to unpack the contents of his school bag. Furthermore, when he sat down, he put his feet up on the desk and folded his arms. Needless to say, his parent had (by this time) disappeared. He ordered me not to touch his school bag because it was his property. I must admit that the day had taken a sharp dip downhill, and things were not looking good. All my good cheer was falling on deaf ears. A further confrontation with him seemed pointless. Power struggle? I had the awful feeling that he had the upper hand!

At this stage, the bell signalled the commencement of class and I did, after all, have a new group of children to attend to. I spoke positively to the children as they listened attentively, with keen enthusiasm etched on their faces. They all looked so refreshed after their holiday. But my challenging young lad wanted to make his presence known. He achieved this by interrupting the class discussion, by badgering me – and other class members – and frequently calling out. To my shock and horror, this was exacerbated by his flat refusal to do anything he was asked. He claimed to have the right to do exactly as he wished.

PRESSING BUTTONS

Calming myself, I decided that I was definitely sending out bad vibrations. How could he possibly be so antagonistic and fired up already? After all it was only

9.15 am day one! I even began to think that maybe I was wearing the wrong deodorant. Was I wearing red? Something was aggravating him! He was certainly trying to press my buttons and test my patience. Was I pressing his?

Whatever the reason, I had to find a way of ensuring he could not repeatedly continue to disrupt us in this manner. Standing close to him, making strong eye contact, speaking quietly but firmly, I asked him to take out his pencil and a book. He barked back at me that he had none and firmly held his desk closed with his knees, and ordered me not to touch his desk. I offered him a piece of paper and a pencil which he repeatedly threw away, but added that I could sharpen the pencil. I repeated my directions firmly and indicated that his behaviour was unacceptable, but he declared that he had had enough and he was leaving.

THE SEARCH

Since I had a whole class of children to attend to, I decided that it was time to contact the principal of the school, who had talked with me about our young lad earlier. When the lad realised that the principal was approaching, he bolted.

People searched for him all day in vain until at 2.50, he boldly waltzed into the classroom, soaking wet. He announced to all that he had only come back to collect his bag. What a wonderful day he had experienced. While we were at school and people had been searching for him, he had spent the day jumping off the Chevron Island Bridge.

THE SLOW CHANGE PROCESS

My colleagues supported me in developing an approach based on team work: setting goals with the child (one-to-one away from the pressure of the 'peer audience'); taking time to talk with him and learn the interests he had (this took time for trust to develop but I 'persisted' – building trust takes time and there is some risk with trust). I also took time to consider his preferred learning style (we do this with all our students). I frequently looked for ways to encourage him and help him build success in his learning.

Above all I had to learn to be patient and kind to myself; realising I couldn't change him – *but I could change how I related to and worked with him*.

PRINCIPLES FOR BEHAVIOUR MANAGEMENT, GROWTH AND UNDERSTANDING

Teamwork

▶ Gain support from the behaviour management team.
▶ Work in collaboration with the parents.
▶ Gain support from other teachers and administration.
▶ Seek advice and support with the consent of parents from Juvenile Aid

Bureau (in extreme cases).
► Gain assistance from counsellors.

Goal setting

► Set firm, clear expectations.
► Provide rewards and appropriate consequences within fair discipline. That discipline was based in class-wide, school-wide, rights, responsibilities, fair rules and consequences. (See Chapter 6.)
► Set small, *attainable*, work goals suited to ability. In this case programmes needed to be modified and the student worked on an *individual* programme.
► Plant the seeds of success – nothing succeeds like success.

Method

► Make contact, connect with the child and take an interest in the child.
► Listen to the child.

Understanding the learner

► Apply the principles of multiple intelligences.
► Encourage the child to learn using his preferred learning style.
► Be flexible – where possible – with learning experiences and modes of assessment.

Trust

► Build trust between child and teacher.

Self-esteem

► Offer encouragement.
► Look for the positives, small though they may seem at first.
► Be enthusiastic in what you say and do – it is contagious and raises the morale of those around you.
► Success breeds success like a rolling stone gathering more and more speed – leading to more and more success.

Your own needs

► Allow yourself to have some fun.
► Be kind and patient with yourself.
► Don't sweat the small things.

GRADUATION (IN TIME!)

My friend completed the year upon the stormy seas. Progress at first was slow and steady, with moderate changes in behaviour. I believe that he began to enjoy many aspects of school life. A great deal of his learning involved 'hands on': constructing, designing, computer work, games, cooking, art and craft and sport. Structure in reading, writing and mathematics proved to be successful. His behaviour remained quite rebellious, particularly with new people, but his anger management did improve.

Outside of school, he achieved success in Scouts and managed the responsibility of a paper run before school. These helped to build his self-esteem. Within the school setting he also accepted monitor positions readily.

REFLECTION

The experience was certainly a challenge, but it is important to acknowledge, as a final thought, the valuable growth that took place within the child and myself, both professionally and personally, as a result of our struggles.

Individual behaviour management plans and group support with infant age children: Troy's story

Debbie Hoy

Debbie is currently headteacher of an infant school in a London suburb. Here Debbie details her journey with a child presenting with 'emotional-behavioural disorder' and how she (with the understanding of her class group) helped Troy. Although these were infant children Debbie was able to engage whole-class (peer) support for this very challenging child. It was this whole-class support, a personal behaviour plan, clear and firm guidelines and unfailing teacher encouragement that helped this young boy change his behaviour. A crucial feature of Debbie's experience with Troy was the unfailing colleague support she received.

TROY'S BACKGROUND

Troy came into my class in September 1995 at nearly six years old for his second year at school. He was a very angry little boy with particularly low self-esteem. He comes from quite a dysfunctional family even though both parents are living in the home. His father cannot read or write and has spent time in prison (fairly regularly) for drug offences. His mum is young and loves Troy in her own way, but finds it difficult to deal with his behaviours, and has trouble disciplining him. She is usually late bringing him to school and he often misses the first session of the day. He also has a sister who is two years younger than him.

I chose to take Troy into my class, knowing that he was challenging in his behaviour and making little progress academically, but also seeing a very sad little boy who had potential.

MAKING A START

The first six weeks of the school year were very challenging. Troy displayed a lot of different types of behaviours, and on some days tested me and the school behaviour policy to the limits. Some days he was quite withdrawn, refusing to do anything much in terms of the curriculum. He would say 'I can't …!' or 'I'm no good at anything!' Most days he would display highly attention-seeking behaviours, trying to make other children laugh at him or notice him. These were the days that were hardest to deal with. He would climb under tables, onto tables, dance around the room instead of lining up, use a very loud voice for almost all conversation, walk 'through' the other children in such a way as to knock into them (to get a reaction, not hurt them), insist on wearing his cap indoors, or on not putting his toys away. During carpet time, he would call out, distract others or play with anything he could touch … The behaviours were many and varied in their frequency and intensity.

I went through the normal pattern of establishing the class as a whole: setting up the rules to support the shared rights, and helping children to take responsibility for their behaviour through a system of choices and consequences. Troy tested the system to see if it was consistent time after time. Some days he responded fairly well to the choices and consequences given to him and would co-operate. On other occasions he would run out of the school, or would become very angry with me and would shout and scream and hit out. At these times, I would sometimes take Troy to another place so that the other children could carry on with their activities, or sometimes it was better to take out the whole of the rest of the class for something special (stickers from the head teacher, an extra playtime, etc.). This had implications for the curriculum for the other children, and also on staffing. Fortunately, I had a full-time teaching assistant in my room who was able to deal with either Troy, or the rest of the class. Sometimes we had to restrain Troy physically. We had a policy on when and how this should be done. It was always carried out with another adult in the room; sometimes in the classroom and sometimes in another room. At first the other children were worried and concerned about his anger and resulting behaviour and we had several class meetings (without Troy) where they could talk about their fears and we role-played different situations so that they felt safe. They quickly learned when to give him appropriate attention and when to 'ignore' his behaviour.

MAKING PROGRESS

Gradually Troy's behaviour began to improve. We worked very hard at increasing his self-esteem by talking about what he is good at and giving him lots of praise and attention for everything we possibly could. This was very time consuming but we could see the pay-off in Troy. His whole manner changed from being a very sullen-looking boy to being a much happier and more smiling child. He learned how to talk to others positively and with a quiet voice, how to sit on the carpet and listen, how to put his hand up without calling out, how to line up quietly and without touching anyone else, how to calm himself down when he felt angry inside, etc. We learned that he found it hard on the days when he was brought to school late to come in quietly and settle into the group which had already got going without him. As adults we often find it hard to walk into a room full of people when we are late. So we helped him by giving him strategies. One of the highlights of the school year was in January when Troy became the 'star of the week' for our class and received his star at assembly.

He wasn't perfect by any means but Troy became a child who enjoyed coming to school and he began to fit into the expected 'normal' patterns of behaviour that we get in any classroom. His behaviour continued to improve with the help of these behaviour 'contracts'. The 'contracts' were based on *learning* the behaviours he needed to be a happier student and improve his learning: behaviours such as 'quiet voice', 'hands up without calling out', 'sitting on the mat', 'keeping hands and feet to yourself', 'facing the front', 'waiting your turn', etc. Unfortunately he still didn't make much academic progress but his self-esteem was getting better all the time and he had lots of extra support from a very talented teaching assistant who managed to relate really well to Troy and get alongside him.

SETBACKS

Everything continued to go well for a few months until about May. Suddenly Troy reverted back to being the child he had been in September (term one in the UK). I found it hard to deal with that and felt that all the hard work we had put into Troy had been wasted. I had expected that it would take a good month at the beginning of the school year to teach Troy the expected patterns of behaviour but after nine months of him being in the class with the routines and relation-ships firmly established I was surprised and very disappointed.

I discovered that his mum was pregnant and Troy had not taken very well to the idea of having another younger sibling. It seemed to be challenging his place in the family and his feeling of being loved and valued. This all came out during a time when I was restraining him with another teacher present. He started shouting out at the top of his voice, 'My mum and dad have two brats already. Lisa (sister) is a brat and now they're having another brat like Lisa' and so on for about ten minutes. It was helpful to know that it was a home influence rather than a school one that had really unsettled him as it explained his behaviour, but we couldn't excuse this behaviour and we had to work on a behaviour recovery plan yet again. The other major thing that happened was that his self-esteem hit rock bottom again; he started to say he was 'no good at anything'.

We continued to tackle Troy's behaviour as we had always done with choices and consequences, 'contracts' and behaviour agreements. The difference this time was that we chose to involve the other children more.

INVOLVING THE CLASS GROUP

I spoke to Troy privately about his behaviour and drew a picture of a ladder (on postcard-sized card) which had a rung for each part of the day. If he behaved appropriately then he had a small 'reward' at the end of the session, or at the end of the morning or afternoon. The rewards were things like stickers, playing with a toy in the head's room for two minutes, then five minutes (building up the time he was allowed throughout the day), trying on a soldier's jacket he had seen in the head's room (a special treat!) and having a go on a special piece of equipment he had seen in the Hearing Impaired Unit. Each day he had a new ladder with the rewards negotiated and written on at the start of each day. At the end of each day if he had had a good day he would get stickers ready *for the rest of the class* and would give them out to the other children.

I held a class meeting for the children about Troy and this time Troy was there. He had agreed to let me talk to the whole class about his daily plans and wanted his classmates to be involved in helping him. I drew a mountain on a big piece of paper and talked (from experience) about how difficult it can be to climb up a mountain. I said that some people find it easy to climb up and want to run on ahead and that some people find it difficult to get up and may need others to help them. Others find it so difficult that they just give up unless they have people encouraging them. As I was speaking, I drew figures on the mountain in different places. Some at the top, others struggling part way up with others helping them. I then spoke about how different people have different 'mountains' in their life. I said that for some of them their 'mountain' was reading, for others it was spelling and writing, for others it was maths, others found sports activities challenging, and for Troy, his 'mountain' was behaviour.

I told the children about Troy's plan and showed them the ladder I had drawn. I asked them to think about ways in which they could help him climb his mountain. We talked about telling him when he was doing something that was good (helpful, thoughtful, kind, working on his class work), ignoring his inappropriate behaviour, reminding him of the rules and giving him two buddies to help him in the classroom and in the playground and several other ideas as well. I told the children that if they helped Troy then at the end of each day they would receive stickers from him if he'd had a good day, or from someone else if he hadn't. We also planned a little visit to the nearby park, a celebration with drinks and biscuits, stickers from the headteacher and so on. I felt that it had to be worth their while to help him or they might not bother, or worse still, some students might copy his behaviour if they felt he had a better 'deal' than them with all the 'rewards' that he would be getting.

After this initial meeting the children were really responsive and supportive. They helped Troy enormously, which in turn helped me too. Another idea that we came up with was to have a message board where we could write positive messages for Troy about the things he did. We drew a picture of him and at different times in the day children went there to write their personal message:

'Troy smiled at me.'
'Troy sat quietly at assembly.'
'Troy did a good picture.'
'Troy used the carpet rules.'

Troy took the message board home with him each time we did this. It became a favourite with the other children and on the days when I forgot to organise it, they got it ready themselves!!

Two class buddies were chosen to help Troy. The two buddies were older children within the class. They were chosen by Troy from a list of suggestions that I gave him. They were very positive with him and firm. I gave them a piece of card with lots of squares on at playtimes so that they could draw smiley faces every time that Troy did something good, thoughtful or kind. They felt that they had some control and responsible power in the situation, which helped them. Troy knew that he had to stay with them at playtime or he would lose his right to go outside.

Troy's self-esteem and behaviour improved enormously over the next few weeks until it was almost back to how he had been earlier in the year. It would be nice to think that the story has finished but I know that after six weeks of school holidays, he'll be coming back into my class with a different mix of children and he will need to re-establish himself in the classroom, what the expected behaviour is, how to belong to the group... and his mum will be having her baby this month too.

COLLEAGUE SUPPORT

One of the key things for me as a teacher has been to know that I have got the support and back-up of the other members of staff. At times during Troy's story probably all of our staff have had to deal with Troy in different situations, shared the load with me, brainstormed new ideas or supported the other children. It has been essential to know that Troy is dealt with consistently across the school by each person and for me to know that I was not alone in the situation.

ENDNOTE

1. Medications such as Dexamphetamine, Ritalin (these are amphetamine-based medications – stimulants). There are also non-stimulant medications used for some types of ADD such as Catapress, Tofronil and Clonadine.

4

The Hard-to-Manage Class:
When it is More Than One or Two

INTRODUCTION

I came across the word *charivari* in an old *Punch* magazine (of the last century). I was intrigued by this word because it appeared on the front cover of the magazine, unexplained. It means 'a serenade of rough music made with kettles and pans or tea trays... used in France in derision of incongruous marriages, hence a babel of music...'. (OSD). Apparently – in this unusual custom – a group of people disturbingly bang tea trays and kettles outside the home of those who the mob believe have occasioned an 'incongruous marriage'(!)[1]

When reading the definition my first thought turned to well entrenched memories of 8D, 9C and 10E! Students noisily forming outside a classroom; pushing, shoving and 'testosteronically bonding' (the male play pushing, shoving, strangling and punching). When physically in the classroom the noise level of the group rises (a minor Babel?); it then takes some time to settle 25 to 30 students prior to a hopeful teaching period. Then the calling out and the talking across the room – while the teacher is seeking to engage whole-class teaching time. Students who walk in late (and some 'grandstand' as they enter); students who 'wander'; noise levels during on-task learning time... Fifty minutes, in a class period, can seem an awfully long time with such a class.

I have worked in many, many classes like this (mainly upper primary, middle-school level). I have worked with colleagues as a teaching mentor; to rebuild a sense of personal goodwill that can easily be eroded when we have such a class on our timetable load! I can easily see why some teachers do not look forward to that class, that day ('do not look forward to' puts it mildly!). Rebuilding goodwill with such a class is not easy when repeated, widespread, distracting (and sometimes disruptive) behaviours seem habituated into the very social fabric of the class. Colleague support is crucial to assist colleagues (as early as possible before *habituated* behaviours become the norm) in rebuilding that goodwill and *sense of shared purpose with the class group* (Rogers, 1997).

In each of the following essays colleagues share how they gained a fresh perspective on the hard-class issue and the approaches they found helpful within the context of no-blame colleague support. Chapter 5 takes these whole-class issues further when it addresses the issues of building co-operative classrooms.

The hard-to-manage class: reasons, options, support

Bill Rogers

Within any classroom group up to 60 or 70 per cent of students are normally willing to co-operate with their teacher in building and sustaining a workable classroom community. In the establishment phase of term one of the school year, this 60 to 70 per cent will quickly habituate behaviour that is consistent with shared rights and responsibilities (Rogers, 1997). This group of students will co-operate if the teacher is respectful, supportive and able to engage the class group with effective teaching and positive, respectful leadership. If, however, the goodwill of this group is diminished by teaching and management that lacks confidence, and conscious and positive structure, it is very difficult to manage that 30 per cent of attentional and challenging students present in many classes. Those students who are emotionally and behaviourally disordered (1 to 5 per cent) are even more difficult to work with if the teacher has lost the goodwill of the majority.

Having worked with many classes at middle school level (grades 5–10) I've noticed that classes *may* become hard to manage for these typical reasons:

- The *particular* mix of students that particular year (a skewed distribution).
- A known 'harder' class has been given to a first year teacher (this is unfair if there is no initial mentoring support). I find I find it professionally untenable when a senior teacher replies with, 'Well that happened to many of us in our first year so why not them?' A *known* hard class should be taken by the more experienced and competent teachers; or, at the very least, there should be a mentor working with that colleague to assist the class teacher to engage the first few lessons (secondary) or first day (primary). The research is clear: *how* the establishment phase of a class is addressed can significantly affect the general cohesion of the class in the weeks ahead (Rogers, 1997).
- The way the class is *characteristically treated* by their teacher significantly affects the co-operative goodwill of the students. If a teacher's leadership style is typically 'bossy', 'petty' (overdwelling on minor issues) or evidencing a negative discipline style it will have a significant effect on learning and behaviour. Mutual respect has to be *mutual*. Conversely, a characteristically non-assertive teaching style will send mixed messages about a teacher's leadership of the group. There are teachers who ignore calling-out, butting-in,

'grandstanding', 'lateness', inappropriate language and banter or inappropriate noise levels. This ignoring of such behaviour may arise out of a misguided hopefulness that things will get better (they won't, not by themselves) or a fear that if they were to firmly confront such behaviours that the students would not actually take any notice. This non-assertive pattern is quickly picked up by students as showing that the teacher cannot manage the situation – or even that they 'don't care'.

▶ Some students with 'attentional' or 'power-seeking' patterns of distracting and disruptive behaviour are not significantly addressed early enough in the first few days and weeks of term one. Such students (particularly those with emotional behavioural disorder such as AD/HD need *early* case-supervision with a conscious focus on individual behaviour plans to teach them the essential behaviours for school life (Rogers, 1997 and 2003a. See also Chapter 3 in this book.).

▶ The most common reason why classes become hard to manage is poor or inadequate establishment *as a class group* in the critical first meetings of week one. Students are psychologically and developmentally ready for their teachers to clarify the necessary rules and routines for learning, behaviour and the relative 'smooth-running' of a complex little community called 'our class' in the very first meetings – term one.

I have worked with many teachers who have not established clear, workable, fair rules and routines on day one to three; have had inadequate seating plans ('Sit where you want guys'); have not established, explained and maintained positive learning and behaviour habits; have not explained, modelled and maintained appropriate noise levels, cues for entry to class and settling time, time-on-task behaviours, etc. Thoughtful establishment also means consistently and fairly following up inappropriate and wrong behaviour after class from the outset – *day one*. Consistent and early follow-up of inappropriate through to challenging behaviour is crucial in the establishment phase of the year. Such follow-up (one-to-one) – whether the 'after-class chat' or formal, due consequences – can be conducted respectfully but with fair certainty to clarify the significance of behaviour ownership in the student.

If teachers do not establish a class group with *conscious* planning, skill, positive leadership and management, the 60 to 70 per cent of normally responsible and co-operative students may covertly – some overtly – collude with the more attentional and challenging students in distracting and off-task behaviours.

WHEN A CLASS HAS SOMEWHAT 'LOST THE PLOT'

When poor patterns of learning and behaviour are 'habituated' across a class group it is essential that the class teacher work with supportive colleagues to de-habituate, and re-habituate positive behaviours. The earlier this is carried out in term one the more effective the process and outcome will be.

If a teacher believes they are 'losing' their class, i.e. if a significant percentage of the class are *frequently*, *generally* and *durably* disruptive (more than bad-day-syndrome) then a 'fresh start' approach is necessary – a re-establishment of the class group to re-engage their understanding, goodwill and co-operation.

FRESH START

A 'fresh start' process (Rogers, 1997) will need no-blame colleague support to produce a workable process and outcome: moral support (not blame) and a willingness by the teacher to work with support colleagues to re-engage the class.

A fresh start process will normally begin with a classroom meeting with the whole class or year group, involving the regular class teacher and a supportive senior colleague (or at least a supportive colleague who has a good working relationship with the class) (see p 68).

This classroom meeting allows an honest appraisal of how things are in the class *at present*. The teacher (with the support of a colleague) needs to utilise the classroom meeting forum as an opportunity for the class group and teacher to address *current behaviour* (of a significant number of students in the class) as it affects learning and relationships. It is important that this meeting is not a lecture or some kind of hectoring verbal pay-back ('I'm sick and tired of this class …!'). Such tirades – obviously – only further alienate the *potential* (and residual) goodwill of the 60 to 70 per cent.

Three key questions my colleagues and I frequently ask of students in such meetings are:

What's working well in our classroom at the moment? (and why?)

What's not working well here at the moment? (and why?)

What can/should we do to change things here? (so that we can get on with having a classroom where we can learn well without undue noise, calling-out, time 'off-task' …).

These questions can be asked through a written proforma, or in an open-forum in a classroom meeting.

The basic rules for all classroom meetings need to be made clear at the outset:

► Focus on the question.
► Constructive responses (no put-downs of *any* class member, including teacher!).
► One at a time and a reasonable time limit (to shared responses and length of meeting).

It can also help to break up the whole class into smaller sub-groups (the 2, 4, 6 method) and then use the whole-class feedback for the whole-class meeting (see Rogers, 1998).

A second meeting will then be called to give feedback and responses to the questions raised at the first meeting. Normally what happens here is that the teacher will list, on a few large posters (and a class hand-out):

► the *behaviours* that cause us all concern
► ways in which we can address and change those issues raised
► the *re-established* rules and routines to support these changes.

The routines often addressed include a change in seating arrangements (to enhance learning time); cues/routines for entry, settling and class learning time (particularly noise levels); cues/routines for engaging teacher assistance (these routines should never be assumed). The earlier in term one that this process of *re-establishment* occurs the more effective will be the long-term outcome.

Some teachers publish the fresh-start outcome as a 'class-plan' (see Rogers, 1997) and in some cases a copy of this is sent home to parents of this class (only after approval by school principal/headteacher).

It can also help (with older students) to publish some positive class posters accentuating core rights and responsibilities, e.g. **We all have a right to learn. To learn well here we**: (then the poster briefly lists the essential, key positive learning rules/routines for this key right and responsibility, e.g. getting to class on time, having our necessary equipment, remember the hands up rule, without calling out, or talking over others, partner-voice during class work time.) **We all have a right to respect here in our class. We show respect when we**: (then list the *essential* aspects of respectful behaviour.)

The published tone of such a plan needs to be positive, constructive, clear and expectant – not simply a list of 'musts' and 'mustn'ts'.

It may be important, too, to encourage some teachers to re-appraise honestly their behaviour leadership and discipline as they embark on any 'fresh start' process with a class group. Goodwill and respect (as noted earlier) is always a two-way street, with significant outcomes dependent of the quality of a teacher's leadership in behaviour management, and thoughtful and fair use of behaviour consequences (see Chapter 6). Most of all the on-going success of a fresh start is affected by the teacher's characteristic use of supportive encouragement and feedback to individual students and the class group. It is never too late to make a fresh start with a class group, providing we are willing to allow personal and professional appraisal, the opportunity for student input, discussion and invitation to co-operate and – most of all – colleague support.

ENDNOTE

1 I also came upon this word in a marvellous book, *Shakespeare's Language* (2000) by Frank Kermode. He suggests that a version of 'charivari' was displayed outside Brabantio's house – interrupting the wedding night of Othello and Desdemona (p. 167).

My most challenging Year 8 class ever

Leanne Wright

In this case study Leanne outlines her experiences with one of her most challenging classes. While they wore her down at times, with colleague support, some reflective planning, good-will and energy she saw a change in their behaviour and learning. Leanne shares the strategies that engaged a 'fresh start' with her class.

I heard about 8D long before I 'picked them up' at the change of semester halfway through the year. Various staff members had thrown up their hands in horror after a lesson spent with them. And even though I must have taught a few hundred grade 8s in my 15 years of teaching I have to say I wondered what had hit me. Every Wednesday afternoon after 100 minutes with just them and me I desperately wanted to resign!

In that class was Rebecca, a girl who had been living on the streets on and off in the last year or so and was only allowed to return home on the proviso that she attended school. There was 'ADD Aaron' who rarely took his medication at lunchtime and whose usual response to being 'told off' was to fart; preferably as loud as possible. I'm sure his diet was designed to produce a smell that would attract lots of attention from his mates who enjoyed the opportunity to 'go bazza'.

We had the elusive Sharon and Cindy who often had to be brought to class after being discovered in their usual wanderings in the corridor 'to find the social worker' or whatever. Angela's upper lip was permanently curled to one side in a sneer that can only be perfected by grade 8 girls. Her mate, Melissa, was nice but easily led. Throw in a handful of extremely low ability kids, some very silly boys, one bored intelligent one and a bright one who kept trying to be moved out of the class because he couldn't stand it, and we had quite an interesting 'cocktail'. I didn't mind the individuals but, boy, at times I hated that class.

Bringing pens and paper to write with was a big problem. I'd always solved that in the past by bringing spares but the other teachers warned me that they never got a thing back, so I named and numbered all my pens and rulers and had a 'library' system recording who everything went to each lesson. That at least worked. (It was pointless trying to get them to give up their own time to solve the failure-to-bring-gear problem – they'd almost never turn up and they'd missed so many detentions it was impossible for senior staff to keep up with it all in supporting the staff, especially since they'd often just nick off or stay away from school.)

Getting them to *use* the pens and paper was an even bigger challenge – except, of course, to write on each other or to 'fight' over. I reorganised my teaching and we did a lot of work on learning social skills in co-operative learning groups. This was chaos at first because it was so different but ultimately I think it helped me to survive with that class. We changed activities about every 15 to 20 minutes from posters to quizzes to try to keep them interested. Unfortunately, I wasn't allowed to take them on excursion because they were known for their shoplifting expertise and their ability to disappear.

I even swallowed my pride and asked senior staff to 'track' them. I'd noticed the shorter morning lesson was nowhere near as bad as the long afternoon one so I asked the senior staff to organise a roster to allow someone to wander through my room a couple of times during the afternoon lesson. It was invaluable. Invariably there was someone for them to chase up or an issue to deal with while I was sorting out something else that was going on and best of all I didn't feel isolated. It didn't always work perfectly though. Sometimes they'd forget and once I ended up with five colleagues in my room at once (they all had found something to deal with while they were there). I thought that was hilarious but I also though it was great – I felt very well supported. All the staff who taught them also had regular case meetings about them to share ideas that had worked for them and to work on common options.

I'd already done a lot of work on classroom rules which I'm sure the kids understood fairly well even though it was more fun doing their own thing. I re-read a book called *You Know the Fair Rule* (Rogers, 1998). A colleague shared an approach with me that was very constructive in helping me to turn that class around. The idea behind it was based on a group incentive system. I went to a local hamburger restaurant and asked them to donate some free hamburgers to my cause – they donated 35 hamburgers and a $5.00 prize. Then I told the kids that to be able to go for lunch with a hamburger for free they had to earn points by supporting our class rules. The 'catch' was they had to earn five points in each category of the rules:

▶ *Communication*, e.g. one person speaking at a time (during class discussions), quiet working voice during classwork time.
▶ *Learning*, e.g. coming prepared for work and letting others learn without disruption.
▶ *Safety*, e.g. not throwing things or hurting each other.
▶ Treating others with *respect*, (e.g. no put downs).
▶ *Movement*, e.g. staying in seats unless it's necessary to move and then doing so in a *sensible* manner.

I put the headings on a sheet and ruled columns up for each lesson – for my purposes it was actually easier to put in a cross if they broke a rule after being reminded, etc. I'd spend a few minutes at the end of the lesson filling in the information (using ticks and crosses for speed). I only gave them a vague idea of their progress at first in order to try to encourage them all. When they had a few ticks and it seemed more achievable I'd tell them how many points (ticks) they had. I found it worked extremely well for the first two weeks but it was a bit too slow (maybe 25 points were too many) and they started to lose interest until I sped it up considerably.

Most of the class managed to get to the hamburger restaurant (although a couple were on suspension for something else – I gave them a couple of burger vouchers when they got back). The ones who didn't make it stayed behind with the senior staff member in charge of my area. She was happy to see the progress made by the others. Meanwhile I got to talk to the kids in a completely different setting – it was really helpful and I'm sure it affected my relationship with them from then on.

Three of the boys in my class got an A on a test I gave them – the first A they had *ever* had! It wasn't an easy test although it was a topic they'd been fairly interested in (buying a car). They just about brought tears to my eyes – they were so thrilled. I also put a piece of work typed up on computer by each class member in a display folder and showed it to the principal. He came to tell me how wonderful it was one day when I was away. When I returned, a few of them came barging excitedly into one of my other classes to tell me that the deputy principal had told them how impressed he was. I would never have believed that success could have actually meant anything to them.

I met up with quite a few of them again on a Year 11/12 orientation day (only about three actually enrolled). It was quite pleasing that they actually seemed to be happy to see me – it highlighted something for me that I've become really aware of over the last couple of years: that the relationship teachers develop with kids is *crucial* to being able to 'do anything' with them.

> *I'm not sure it was the actual strategy that I used with 8D that made the difference, but the fact that it made for a more positive atmosphere and better relationship building.*

Another comment I'd like to make is that I'm amazed at how much learning it is possible to do in the area of behaviour management. I've been teaching for 16 years and am still putting new things into practice – I'm still reflecting on what it means to be a teacher.

I'll never forget that class and the rewards I gained from taking a few risks. I thought I might be seen as a hopeless teacher by asking for help and chaos reigned at times as I experimented in order to get them to do something constructive. I'm really just glad that I survived at all!

P.S. I never could totally eliminate Aaron's farting.

The 'class from hell'

Denise Frost

Seven years ago Denise experienced 'the class from hell'. She was a new teacher to the school and several weeks into second term. It was a grade 3: 8 to 9-year-olds (7 girls and 14 boys). The class was causing a lot of concern for all the staff members. The expectation from the principal was to settle this very restless and challenging class – 'learning' was 'secondary'.

In this essay Denise shares the frustration and stress that very challenging class behaviour can bring – even to experienced teacher leadership. With reflective colleague support and a dogged goodwill that re-engaged the children, Denise saw the class change for the better over time.

When I walked into the classroom, the children had taken an instruction from their previous teacher to 'sit anywhere' quite literally. Desk placement had no uniformity, some even facing away from the blackboard to look out windows or onto blank walls. The first day was discipline, discipline and more discipline. One sum and more discipline.

BEGINNINGS

I began my first teaching day with, 'What sort of day do we want?', 'How can we achieve it?'

Very basic classroom rules were established, e.g., 'listen and eyes this way in instructional time', 'hands up', 'one person speaking at a time', 'stay in seats', etc.

Each day ended with, 'What kind of day did we have?', 'What went well?', 'What didn't?' Then 'the slate' was wiped. Each day began with a clean slate and a class conference. 'What kind of day do you want today?' 'Who can make that happen? How?' Through these 'conferences' I was inviting the students to take some shared control with me of *our* class.

There were one or two ringleaders among several 'challenging' students. I roved the room with a notebook to record names of students I needed to follow up and those who needed time-out (I did not rely on my memory).

I encountered many challenging behaviours, more than often all on one day: calling out, roving students, work refusal, breaking pencils and throwing books, sulking and swearing, up-turning desks, bullying and running away.

STRATEGIES

Some of the strategies I used in my time with these students (from *You Know the Fair Rule*, Rogers, 1998) were:

▶ Daily meetings first up to begin the day positively, and also at the close of our day together.

▶ Remaining as 'calm' as possible (especially when replacing the up-turned desks and broken pencils).

▶ Planning for the daily disruptions – with clear routines and reminding of rules without arguing, like teaching to *focused* students by waiting for the majority to be attentive; acknowledging positive behaviours as much as possible (even hands up) and giving encouragement whenever possible (and the children loved stickers).

▶ Giving short-term learning goals (10 minutes then finally half an hour).

▶ Making contracts (behaviour contracts for ringleaders and those with behaviour needs), giving clear choices (work now or make up time later) and having a supportive time-out plan (colleague support was fantastic here).

OUTCOMES

By the end of the year, thanks to colleague support over those challenging months, the class was starting to work well. Behaviour improved with an added bonus that learning had taken place – two sorts of learning:

▶ real learning (about what it means to get on with each other, as a class, *day after day*)

▶ the academic learning.

The *real* learning was the most gratifying. These students who had earlier displayed little self-control were now able to discern the impact of their actions on a class and to modify their responses to make a difference.

On the last day during our reflection time, one student responded for all when he said, 'We've come a long way Miss. Remember the first day, we only got one sum done. Now look at what we get done in a day! It's great!'

The class agreed they liked it so much better this way and recognised that they, in their choice of behaviour responses, had made the difference.

Classroom meetings to the rescue

Carmen Price

Many teachers have successfully used classroom meetings and friendship circles to support positive behaviour management. Carmen Price shares how she has utilised such approaches to enable conflict management, problem solving and repairing and rebuilding among students. In this primary classroom Carmen was able to encourage the classroom – as a learning community – to reflect on, and take charge of, their behaviour.

THE SCENE

It was the beginning of term 3 (often one of the hardest terms to get through) and a class of Year 4 students were becoming increasingly disruptive and challenging. This class was recognised throughout the school as one of the most difficult compositions of Year 4 students. They shared a demountable building with another group of Year 4 students who were also far from being 'angels'. The noise in the classroom often reached deafening limits as Jack complained about someone taking his pencil, Anne cried because she hadn't had a turn on the computer, Billy tapped his desk with his ruler just because he felt like it, and a low hum filtered through the air as children chatted and complained to their neighbours. Of course there was also the fact that this class contained a large proportion of children with learning difficulties, most of them also displaying a variety of challenging behaviours and experiencing many social and emotional difficulties outside the school setting.

For the first semester the children had very much been in the 'forming' and 'norming' stages of group development. Many new students had joined the class, some children had moved class and the children were getting acquainted with a new teacher. However, by third term the class was in full swing – 'storming' had begun and it seemed like they would never perform. Needless to say, the teacher was at her wits end. She had struggled long and hard to understand the needs of each of these children and had suffered beyond the call of duty. Tried and trusted teaching and management techniques, individual interventions, provision of school support (learning support, teacher assistance time), regular yoga classes and frequent holidays were not proving enough to get through this school year.

A CLOSER LOOK

At first glance the situation seemed overwhelming. The givens were that the class composition could not be altered and that some circumstances beyond the school environment could not be controlled or modified (families will break down regardless of efforts made). However, at closer inspection many positives and much potential existed. In the early stages the teacher had worked hard to create clear expectations for the class. There was evidence that rules, rights and responsibilities for the classroom had been established. Reward and consequence systems were also in place; in fact, the teacher had gone to great lengths to use appealing and creative processes to motivate and regulate the students' behaviours. There were 'praise cheques', sticker books, bottle-top token economies, 'bank books' and positive points to recognise appropriate actions. More challenging behaviours were managed through 'steps' processes (e.g. Warning ⇒ Quiet Time ⇒ Time Out ⇒ Office), the chill-out corner and being on 'probation'. This class was filled with a wealth of behaviour management ideas, and yet there seemed to be a lack of co-operation and cohesiveness. The teacher was feeling utterly exhausted with trying to keep up with curriculum demands and the follow-through of the classroom behaviour management plan. Tension was mounting, and would grow worse by the end of the week, after lunch breaks, after specialist lessons (or any other change in usual schedule) and when environmental conditions changed, e.g. it got hot, it rained, full moon(!), etc.

HELP IS AT HAND

All this did not go unnoticed and a more holistic approach prevailed. Strategies were implemented to control some of the environmental factors. For example, dividers were installed between the classes to cut down excess noise and some boundaries were more clearly established to cut down interference from in-coming calls during teaching time. However, the provision and acceptance of colleague support was to make a real difference and generated different ways to view and handle this situation, and most importantly illustrated that *no one is alone in these situations*. I am sure we can appreciate what it is like to have a class just like this one or to have nightmares of such a class!

Together the teacher and her support colleague began to gather information and collaborate. By putting the evidence together it became apparent that the teacher was carrying much of the responsibility for the classroom functioning. While the behaviour management strategies were creative and abundant, there had been limited student involvement in these processes. With such a variety of strategies in place it was also becoming difficult to implement and follow through with all of them effectively. Rules, rights and responsibilities once clearly displayed about the classroom had also slipped to the sideline as the class became more and more difficult to manage.

The students were also relying on the teacher to solve every little problem that was raised. Jeff would complain that Ben took his pencil, Ben would say that someone tripped him over, Kate would whinge that she couldn't work because the boy beside her was talking and Sally would continually ask what she should do when she was finished. Children would approach the teacher mid-sentence with seemingly minor problems without any attempt at finding their own solution. Even though the teacher tried using reminders and prompts to encourage the students to attempt to solve their own problems or follow class processes (e.g. 'What have you tried so far to work this out?' 'What is our rule in this classroom for asking questions?'), the frequency of these types of behaviours was so great that it often was easier to take on the responsibility to solve the student's problems (e.g. 'Give Jeff back his pencil Ben!'). However, it was important to remember that every student in this classroom had some responsibility for its functioning. This was the aim – we sought to realise that aim by more directly involving the students as a class group.

THE CHANGE PROCESS

It was decided to start with the least intrusive way to influence what was occurring in the classroom. The question was asked: What is the least we can do to make a difference with these kids? Many strategies and techniques had been tried, so what now? It was a process that came to the rescue. A process that could give some of the responsibilities of managing the classroom functioning to the students. A process that could help the children learn how to solve problems on their own, a technique promoting self-reflection and internal motivation. The decision was made to facilitate a class meeting and to use this process as a vehicle for change. While this was not a new phenomenon to this class, it was a different approach to the usual meetings where the teacher addressed issues of concern with the class and explored logical consequences.

The teacher and the support colleague were to conduct the class meetings together. It was decided that the teacher would facilitate the meetings with her colleague beside her as 'a visitor' watching how the classroom worked to solve problems. This was to help to empower the teacher's role in the classroom. Furthermore, the teacher would be the one (together with the students) implementing the ideas generated from the class meetings and therefore should be the one to initiate and implement this change process.

THE CLASS MEETING

The process for the class meetings was based on the ideas presented in the books *Cracking the Hard Class* (1997) and *Behaviour Recovery* (1994) by Bill Rogers. A lot of energy was put into 'advertising' the first class meeting. Invitations were given to each student and flyers were sent home to explain the idea to parents. It was hoped that this would gain the students' interest and create the expectation that this was something new and different to the norm.

By the first class meeting the children were eager and interested. The first meeting took place at the beginning of the week in the morning. This was aimed at establishing the idea of a 'fresh start' to the week (and to the year from the teacher's point of view!). Students were encouraged to sit in one large circle (away from their desks and the usual formality of the classroom), on the same level as the teacher. The class meeting was to be seen as a time for everyone to get together as a team. A time limit was set for the first meeting and a brief description was given on the purpose of class meetings. The teacher explained that it would be a time for group discussion on problems that were bothering the class. She explained that it would be a time for everyone to speak openly and to share their thoughts, opinions and ideas. The teacher then asked for students' thoughts on having frequent class meetings. The class agreed it would be a good idea. During this meeting the class was on-task and focused.

The first meeting established some class meeting rules (with input from most students) and other processes for running the meetings. One thing that was decided upon was the use of a 'talking stick' in the meetings so that only one person would speak at a time (the person holding the stick). It was also decided that an 'issues board' would be used during the week to record any ideas for decision at the next meeting. The general framework for each meeting was based around the following questions:

What is working well in this class (for you, for all of us) and why?
What is not working so well and why?
What can we do to improve things or make things better?

After each prompt, time was allowed to share observations and concerns, test out opinions, share ideas and look for solutions (evaluating the positives and negatives of each).

In the beginning, meetings were conducted twice a week as there were many issues that the class wanted to discuss. It also seemed important that the class received regular feedback on progress towards set goals. The teacher had the main role as facilitator during the meetings with the goal to model the process to the students. As time progressed meetings became less frequent (once a week or upon request if an issue was raised) and teacher input became more subtle as students became familiar with the process and took on the key roles of facilitation. Students also progressed from addressing more problem-focused topics like classroom behaviour plans and peer conflicts in the classroom and playground, to more educational topics like wanting to learn social skills, conflict resolution skills and peer mediation skills.

These meetings became a regular feature of classroom life.

THE OUTCOME

The class meeting process seemed to illustrate to the children that they were valued, involved and key participants in class life. It helped them to see that they and their concerns, ideas and opinions counted – they 'belonged' in the classroom. The meetings also led to a more peaceable classroom environment with simplified reward and consequence systems and redefined rules, rights and responsibilities. It also became a forum for enlisting class support for understanding and working with more challenging students. Most importantly the class meetings achieved outcomes that were agreed to by all the students and the teacher.

It would be nice to claim that this story ended happily ever after, yet in the real world we know that challenges are a natural part of our daily lives – life would be boring without them. Hence the Year 4 class did struggle from time to time with issues they brought with them to school and still on the odd occasion approached the teacher for help with solving their problems. Yet this can be expected with students in this stage of development and in a society that relies a great deal on external approval and control. It is pleasing to say that by the end of term 4, the students were well and truly 'performing' as a team, were being more responsible for their own choices and actions, and were also achieving more curriculum outcomes through a more positive attitude toward the teacher *and* their learning.

The 'icing on the cake', so to speak, occurred at the 'parent day' – a day when the parents visited their children's classrooms to see some of the achievements of the year. On this day the students got to facilitate their own class meeting in front of the parents to illustrate how their class 'worked things out'. The positive response from the parents was overwhelming, with many parents commenting that it would be wonderful if they could use such an idea at home (e.g. family meetings) to solve problems. This feedback was valued by both the teacher and students – it confirmed what they already knew about all they had accomplished as a team.

At first glance, some people would have given up on this Year 4 class; however, a caring and dedicated teacher, a team approach to intervention and a group of children willing to change moved this class towards positive outcomes. While it took hard work from everyone involved, the results and the learning experiences along the way made it all worthwhile.

Can you believe that it was hard to say goodbye to this group of children on the last day of school? What a journey it was!

A *winner* – in a *hard class*

Heather Fraser

Heather Fraser details the journey of her relationship with a 'class from hell' – in particular a nine-year-old boy whose window-climbing exits and expletives and much more were a challenge. Meeting that challenge required some teacher soul-searching, time and patient goodwill.

Heather honestly shares the frustrations of what can often feel like a 'treadmill' when a small but significant number of students seem to hijack a class. Heather shares how 'focused time' and colleague support helped make a difference to these children.

Have you ever had the class from hell?. You know the one. How could you forget? The one that is over-size in numbers, well nourished with gratification-type foods, tending to be also over-size in big-headedness, the 'Let's stir things up and get lots of attention' (of the negative type).

How can you forget the body language of some of the children that says 'I am so cool in my latest gear', 'School sucks', 'I don't want to be here', 'I am doing you a favour when I actually do the set work expected from me' and 'It's fun to interact with me mates around the room'. The latter being a euphemism for the friendly interaction of throwing comments and insults around the room. Then there is the sport of 'How many times can we interrupt the teacher when she is explaining things?' Not a scene conducive to other than survival teaching for a newcomer to a grade in term 4, regardless of her copious amounts of experience.

Now if you have all that in your memory, don't leave out the two students who stand out over and above the others – and of the two, one not interested in any 'learning' at school, it seems, and the other the ringleader who sets his mate off, which in turn can set off the rest of the class!

It was this type of scenario I inherited in term 4 some few years ago. I took over this grade 4, enabling the class teacher to go on a well deserved long service leave. I had not long returned from extended leave overseas. Bad news always travels quickly and I had certainly heard of this group. In particular, Johnny, nine years old, very unkempt in appearance, out of uniform most of the time, always grubby and his hands covered in leaking biro (he didn't have his pen licence because of the poor standard of his handwriting, though he managed to have biros to suck and chew).

71

JOHNNY – A CHALLENGING STUDENT

Johnny was constantly in trouble. He spent most of his days in the principal's office or some other time-out venue. He would clear off home, some distance away from the school, if he could 'escape', which he tried on at least one occasion, cutting through the fly wire screen in the time-out room and attempting to scramble out of the window. On this occasion, only because there were staff covering every exit, he did not succeed but he did manage to call everyone within hearing distance rude names to make your ears curl!

Johnny was on the dreadful treadmill of 'anything that goes wrong is my fault'. His peers would easily and happily send blame in his direction and it so easily stuck! There was a high level of antagonism between him and most of his peers, both in class and in the playground. This boy's self-esteem and recognition was built on getting attention and always of the punitive kind. His body language strongly reflected a 'don't care' attitude. There was rarely any eye contact and he really only spoke in short incomplete sentences, his head down.

Book work was almost non-existent. What he did produce was scrappy, illegible, incomplete, inaccurate, grubby and he often failed to start because he couldn't find his pencil. Not being able to locate a writing implement was a matter of course at the beginning of each session, not each day but every time he needed to do some application work. With this being the case, it was difficult to ascertain Johnny's academic ability. His quick-wittedness with 'smart alec' comments, his cunningness in covering himself concerning trouble, what he could actually do as seen with the limited amount he did do under supervision led me to believe that Johnny could learn, could be a competent learner, but his frequent pattern of task-avoidance was making this outcome seemingly unachievable.

At this point I need to add that he was a very disorganised person. His desk was a nightmare: papers everywhere, torn and screwed up and nothing in their folders; exercise books ripped; felt-tip pens loose and without lids causing more mess; bits of old lunch; hats (non-school hats) and old jumpers; other 'flotsam and jetsam' peculiar to nine-year-old boys and sometimes that elusive pen and pencil we couldn't find. It was little wonder it took so long for him to get started.

My years of teaching experience and student management led me to believe this boy had backed himself into a big hole and was out of his depth on many fronts. It was not too difficult to work out that his frustrating behaviour was avoidance behaviour and the avoidance was a further cover for a number of obvious and not so obvious issues.

STARTING TO HELP JOHNNY CHANGE HIS FOCUS – WORKING TOGETHER

It is always difficult to devote more time to someone in your class who already takes up huge amounts of your time, even if it is for purely discipline reasons. But the first step was to help with the seemingly absent organisation skills – that is, after I had positioned him in the class where he had no eye contact with certain other students and in the midst of students who had good self-discipline so they wouldn't be too distracted by him.

So, to begin with, each morning recess I stayed back with him for several minutes to help clean out his desk, sometimes finding the 'lost pencil' and getting the next books needed to the top of the pile. This was a consequence of his wasting time in the first session and, therefore, not being able to find anything. Over time, probably because of the daily desk clean out and finding things in his desk by himself, Johnny became more successful in his learning tasks and in his learning focus. My individual attention (seen as positive) and time was appreciated, although I only realised this when over the three months period he was slightly more relaxed with me and slightly more co-operative. Besides, this lad was missing out on some of his recess time, in itself a nuisance for him and me, but, in my case, in the long run, well worth it. Regarding the constant loss of pencil, he had to hand it in to me before he went to play, lunch and home. The task for me was to remember to collect it because it was up to me to follow through to be effective.

The next bit of extra time from me (besides the necessary discipline) was to station myself near him or regularly moving back to stand beside him and direct and encourage him to the next item. I would even get him started by doing the first item with him. I am afraid there probably is no other way, no short-cut or less teacher-intensive way – and I was fairly quickly rewarded in seeing a quantity and quality of work completed.

It must be noted that I was not setting unachievable goals like completing all the set work (or in the early period, even half of it!). We were coming from virtually no output to some. I would be grateful for any change, no matter how small at first – but in the longer term, aiming as high as I dared. I was encouraged and my delight must have showed, as Johnny began to respond. In the meantime there were another 29 fourth-graders busily doing 'their thing'. Johnny wasn't the only distracting or disruptive student.

The days that Johnny didn't come to school – I must admit – were blissful. We were pretty much a normal energetic grade 4. However, there were very few of those days when Johnny was not there.

My principal was most supportive, encouraging me to send Johnny to him to give me some relief and restore some form of sanity to the classroom, but my pride and my self-esteem in terms of student management got the better of me most of the time. However, I did relent once or twice; after all, the students would benefit and so would I. I only had this class for the last term so I guess you could consider me 'fresh'. As I would not easily or quickly send him out he realised this was where he was to be – in our class, not merely getting out of things.

JOHNNY IN GRADE 5 – MAKING PROGRESS

When it came to student placement for grade 5, I was to have a grade 5 so I volunteered to have Johnny – yet again – and surprisingly no one objected! The fact was I was seeing a glimmer of hopefulness that 'the worm had turned' but one term was not enough to cement it and for some reason I felt another year would be more enduring. To help even further our principal decided to break the three groups of big classes of over 30 into four smaller groups. I had a tiny room and, now, 23 students. This made an enormous difference. As well as smaller numbers for each class, the challenging students had more individual attention, and lost some of their 'punch'. That previous grade 4 level was heavy duty. You seem to get that every now and again in a school's history. This demonstrated the importance of grade size and student structure. It turned out that I didn't need to enforce the kind of focused and firm discipline needed the previous year in grade 4. The four new grade 5 teachers were extremely grateful for this rearrangement.

Teaching grade 5 was a breeze for the reasons I have mentioned. The smaller class size and a dispersion of personalities also contributed positively to Johnny's behaviour. That was the year when, by accident (or fortunate opportunity), we saw another side to him. He was happier in the smaller class setting; he knew me as a helper (from last term) and the students who had reinforced his innappropriate behaviour were no longer in the same class. Also, with a smaller class and far more relaxed environment, we did more interactive and interesting things like formal debating (not the arguing with the teacher variety as in the past). It was here we saw another skill. This boy, who thrived on positive attention (like most of us), could get this undivided attention through debating, and his previously mentioned quick-wittedness became a positive attribute. I would often find him in a corner, by himself, reciting what he wanted to say before beginning a debating session.

He further came into his own when the class started practising for the annual school concert. It became a public way of showing all his peers and the whole school community a most talented side of a boy who in the past seemed to think the only way to get attention was the negative kind. At the dress rehearsal some of the cast were absent, causing last minute panic. Without direction, Johnny – who had learnt all the roles – stepped into the various characters, saving the day!

I don't wish to suggest that this was 'magic'; there isn't any. It was about limit setting, defining the expectations (probably considered 'barriers' by the student), taking small achievable steps, *regularly* encouraging the child and in doing so allowing success – slowly turning the focus round. Once there is some positivity, the feeling of success, there is a chance to find something the child is good at and helping them to capitalise on this.

Family support is essential and early in grade 5 I did point out to his parents the wonderful changes we were noticing and sought their support. Daily reading and homework commitments were basically my theme with them and a noticeable change was seen outside the classroom. As my influence 'dimmed' there was still improvement in Johnny's consistency and loyalty.

On the occasions when, as with most children, I had to bring back their attention, all I needed to do with Johnny now was to look (and not my 'fierce version' either.) Gone were the days when disciplining him meant anger, denial and abuse. The nice thing was he would usually either give me a grin or say sorry and *get on with his work*.

This was wonderful for me as a teacher. As far I was concerned all was normal. I should add that structured school work was usually completed without much of my intervention. Johnny still had some trouble using his initiative with tasks like projects by the end of year 5. While he tended to stay at the job, planning was still his weakness unless a structure was agreed upon. I expected this would improve with a little maturity and when he moved into grade 6.

During his year in grade 5 Johnny's humour and quick-wittedness won him over with his class peers and he found new friends. Also the fact that the students in our class saw that I had time for this lad, indicating he was not a 'lost cause', must have influenced them to develop a better attitude towards him. Johnny began to look people confidently in the face when talking to them. He was also more consistent with his school uniform – with a little help from a friend (the principal). He only had a few lapses.

FINALLY

To summarise, I guess when the need is great, we find that hidden reserve of patience and doggedness. Most essential, and I cannot emphasise this enough, it is essential to be prepared to put in the time for the student: set realistic goals, be fair and consistent and follow up, follow up on everything – the good and the not so good. Once Johnny saw that I was out to help him and at the same time there were fair limitations for behaviour in our class and fair consequences, he learned to trust and change. (I knew I had really reached him when he felt comfortable enough to call me Mrs F.)

Johnny moved on to grade 6 (without my influence) to retain a reasonably calm demeanour, doing well throughout his grade 6 journey. Yes, he had the odd detention but took it without argument, faced his consequences and moved on. He stood there at the Grade 6 Graduation Ceremony, receiving his certificate just like every other kid – happy, proud, special and in his case with an inkling of gratitude. He had made it – in more ways than one.

Don't underestimate the power of a teacher to influence your students!

5

Working to Build a Co-operative Classroom Group: Classroom Meetings and Building Relationships

INTRODUCTION

Classroom meetings have been widely used in schools for many years. But a classroom meeting as discussed here is more than a normative classroom discussion, it is a structured format – a process – allowing students a *guided voice* on issues of common concern to them as individuals and as a group.

Here is what one whole-class *classroom* behaviour agreement says about their meetings:

In our class, grade 6, we use classroom meetings for various purposes such as playing games, discussion activities, planning and as a way of discussing and solving problems.

The classroom meeting is open to everyone in our class and everyone has the right to express their feelings or to remain silent. Sometimes we invite students from other classes into our classroom meetings.

These meetings are positive and constructive, trying to help and support the individual whilst dealing effectively with the problem. We always try to make the person feel supported and understood at the end of a problem solving discussion.

Any consequences that are discussed by the children at these meetings must be real activities, related to the problem and respectful to the children.

The teachers writing the following essays use classroom meetings help their students to:

▶ understand other students' feelings and concerns (perspective taking)
▶ test out their individual views
▶ widen their own understanding of what others believe and value
▶ see where there is clear consensus on common concerns, feelings and needs
▶ develop communication skills and problem-solving skills. In each of the case examples shared by teachers their aim is to *lead* the classroom group not

'take it over'. It is important that the teacher sets fair rules and guides the agenda then encourages and supports the students in *their thinking processes*. I have seen 'classroom meetings' fail because teachers use such meetings to inform, 'tell' or merely control student thinking.

▶ gain confidence in communicating one's views and feelings to others
▶ meet basic needs such as belonging, fun and enjoyment.

In primary schools – notably – such a format is often part of weekly process in the life of a class. One of the wider goals of such meetings is to build a mediation culture in schools, supporting students to problem-solve and mediate where possible. Such groups can enable teachers to hear their students' 'voice' in a focused way; to value that voice and guide and support that voice within shared rights and responsibilities.

Friendship problems: using a solving circle

Carmen Price

A group of five girls in Year 6 were referred by the classroom teacher for some difficulties maintaining effective friendships. The girls had received several detentions for 'fighting' (displaying verbal and physical aggression) with each other, and parents had started to express their concern regarding these girls playing together. Efforts were made by the teacher and parents to reason with the girls to 'stay away from each other' and 'choose other friends'. Consequences had also been put in place if the girls were seen together (e.g. playground passes, time in planning room). Yet, these strategies (based on external control) proved to have little impact. The move was made to look at other ways to improve the relationship between the girls rather than aiming to extinguish the friendship altogether.

INTERVENTION PROCESS

With some background information on the girls and their issues I began to plan the intervention process. While I would have to negotiate meeting times and the like with the group of girls, the school was prepared for me to work with the group for at least an hour each week over three or four consecutive weeks. Additional time was allocated for follow-up support with the teacher so that she could encourage the girls to practise any new skills in their natural environments. The intervention process was based on the 'Choice Theory/Reality Therapy' approach (Glasser, 1992), utilising Glasser's concept of the 'solving circle' (SC) as the key intervention tool.

The 'solving circle' idea has been typically used as a marriage counselling technique; however, it can be adapted and applied with clients experiencing other forms of relationship challenges. The SC process asks five key questions:

1 *Do you want to help your relationship?*
2 *Whose behaviour can you control?*
3 *What do you believe is wrong with the relationship now?*
4 *What do you believe is good about the relationship now?*
5 *Tell me one thing you could do that would make the relationship better.*

It is based on the notion that the relationship is separate to any individual opinion or want in the group. Those involved in this process are prompted to physically step inside the SC if they want to work on improving the relationship (this may involve visualisation of a circle around them or moving into a designated area). Once inside the SC the relationship can begin to be more reflectively understood and the process of rebuilding given potential.

Before meeting with the girls I considered the visual tools I would use to introduce the idea of the SC. Since I knew the girls individually (from working within their classroom) I had already established some rapport and the foundations of a trusting relationship.

SESSION 1

The girls arrived as scheduled. I had arranged some seats in a circle and I encouraged the girls to take a seat. It was interesting to note the seating position each girl chose. The dynamics of the group were already becoming apparent. The perceived 'leader' of the group took a seat at one end of the circle (opposite me) and the remainder of the group seemed to split into two sections.

We went around the group and briefly introduced ourselves. I then asked the girls the reason they thought they might have been approached to see me. The group looked towards the leader for a response. The response was simple: 'We keep fighting and our parents don't want us to be friends any more' and then, 'If T wouldn't keep annoying us we wouldn't fight so much'. The blame cycle had begun just as I had suspected. I did not give this last comment any energy.

I continued by informing the girls that I knew everyone had been trying to keep the girls apart and that it hadn't really been very successful or helpful, so we were going to try something different. I was there for their 'friendship', not to take sides with anyone but to work for their 'friendship'. I wrote the word 'friendship' on the whiteboard as if it were a separate entity and pointed at this word every time it was mentioned. I then said to the girls that I needed to know a few things before we could go on with helping the 'friendship' and that we would spend the session finding out these things.

I emphasised the importance of the first question and then asked each girl: '**Do you want to help your friendship?**' The common response was, 'If she wants to help it' and 'only if everyone else does', so I restated my question again. 'This is just about what *you* want. Regardless of what the other girls say, do *you* want to help your friendship?' After some time to consider the girls responded 'yes'. I congratulated them for getting through the first difficult question, and stated that I, too, wanted to work on their friendship – we had a common goal. My aim was to put a lot of energy into setting this first question up and the idea of the 'friendship' being separate to any one of them and their personal needs.

I then continued on with the question: '**Whose behaviour can you control?**' To avoid the same people responding all the time, I directed this question to a different member in the group. All girls were able to reach the conclusion that they could only control their own behaviour. This may reflect learnings attained within the school setting, which has adopted a 'Choice Theory' approach (Glasser, 1986).

I then asked the third question: '**What do you believe is wrong with the friendship now?**' This prompted a whirlwind of blame (which I expected). I managed the exchange of this information with brief acknowledgments and redirection to the next person. Of course, there were a variety of reasons (e.g. 'She goes off and plays with other people', 'She bosses us around', 'They whisper about me', 'They leave me out of their games'). Yet these reasons were not what I wanted to focus on.

I was more interested in their response to the next question, and so I asked: '**What is good about your friendship now?**' The girls could each mention a few points (e.g. 'We look out for each other', 'We share with each other', 'We play fun games together', 'You always have someone to hang around'). This led on to brainstorming more general ideas (recorded on the whiteboard) about what makes a friendship good (i.e. friendly actions, words, etc.). I chose to extend this question a little further by asking: 'What do people *do* or *say* when they are being friendly?' I thought that this question might help the girls to consider what 'friendly behaviours' actually looked and sounded like.

This then lead on to the final question: 'Tell me one thing you could each do that you think may make your friendship better?' I referred them to the ideas on the board to assist them in generating a goal. Each girl could come up with one thing with little effort. As they mentioned their idea, I got them to stand and step into the SC (which we called the 'Friendship Circle') that I had drawn on the floor with the word 'Friendship' written in the middle. Once we were all inside the circle I explained the concept of the SC and explained that while they chose to be inside the circle they were choosing to work on the friendship and what they themselves could do to improve it (as they can only control themselves). The girls liked this concept and asked if they could take the word 'friendship' away with them in case they needed to use 'the circle' during the week. The session finished with each group member having a 'friendly' behaviour to practise for the week and one more to think of and bring back to the next group meeting.

At the end of the session I felt as though several goals had been achieved. The girls had gained more information on the concept of 'control' and whom this extends to (ourselves). They had a better idea of the SC, and they were working to improve the friendship rather than trying to change individual aspects of the group. Over the following week I helped the girls to use the circle in the school setting and rehearsed this process with the teacher (who was helping the girls to apply the SC in the ordinary, day-to-day environment).

SESSION 2

The first session had focused on setting up the SC process and introducing the girls to the concepts behind this process. Over the next week the girls had tried to apply the SC idea on their own and had experienced some difficulties in doing so. The classroom teacher had reported that the girls were approaching her with complaints that some girls would not step into the circle and were causing fights in the group. From this feedback it became apparent that the girls were still stuck on the idea of external control (forcing others to get into the circle) and needed more practice with the ideas of 'Choice Theory' and the SC. The focus of session

2 was to review the week's progress and the goals they had set themselves, and to work with any challenges or positives experienced over the week.

The girls did not arrive at the session together (even though they were sent from the same class). Two girls arrived promptly and two others lingered behind. The group once again sat as though they were 'split' with a large space between the girls. Once seated the girls launched into explanations of the week, which mostly contained blaming and complaints about other girls not stepping into the circle (e.g. 'We were having some trouble getting along and T wouldn't step into the circle to work it out. It was all her fault'). I worked to reframe their thinking by asking the girls, 'Who can you control?' Each girl responded 'Myself'. I followed this with a reflection like 'It sounds to me that some of you may have forgotten this, and were trying to control or get other people to step into the SC – maybe that was part of the problem you were having. Does that sound like what was happening?' Most girls nodded in agreement. With the process underway and the framework for thinking and behaving redefined the session progressed more smoothly.

We reviewed the week by revisiting the goals set and used a 10-point scale to consider each girl's journey towards improving the friendship. The points on the scale reflected behaviours that we would see or hear if they were moving towards improving the friendship or in contrast moving away from the relationship. On occasions I had to remind the girls that I was there for the friendship rather than any individual person. We practised using the SC and considered what we would do if people did not want to enter the SC. I highlighted to the girls that if they chose to stay outside the SC they were still required to follow the school guidelines for getting on with others (in other words being outside the SC did not give them the right to be unfriendly). There were rights, rules and responsibilities at school about how people should treat others regardless of the closeness of their relationships. I also pointed out the natural consequence if the girls chose to act in unfriendly ways. My goal in presenting this information was to ensure that the girls were not using the SC as a means to justify their actions (e.g. 'I was not in the SC on the day I teased her'). They had to understand the rights, rules and responsibilities within the school setting too. The session ended with each girl choosing one way they could help the friendship over the next week.

SESSIONS 3 TO 5

The next few sessions were of shorter duration. The girls started to arrive together (rather than split) which seemed to indicate that the relationship was improving. These sessions involved further practice using the SC, setting goals for change and deeper probing into areas of difficulty using 'Reality Therapy' techniques (e.g. 'What were you hoping would happen when you chose to say something nasty to T?', 'What did you do to get what you wanted?' , 'Did that choice help the friendship or harm the friendship?'). We also regularly used the 10-point scale to review outcomes and the group's movements towards its goal to improve the friendship.

Further intervention involved practising the use of the SC in the girls' everyday environment and collaborative consultation with the classroom teacher.

Towards the end of the five sessions the girls indicated that they had reached around a '7' on the 10-point scale. A score of '7' indicated the use of friendly behaviours like sharing, taking turns, speaking openly, and using respectful and friendly words and actions to one another. This score was a long way from the original response that showed behaviours like teasing, using put-downs, fighting and spreading rumours. The SC process seemed to have assisted the girls in changing their relationship with one another for the better. While outside assistance was still needed from time to time to help the girls to work on some of their relationship problems, the teacher, parents and administration were pleased with the progress of the relationship between the girls, and were happy for the relationship to continue.

In several 'booster sessions' that followed, the teacher and I assisted the girls in dealing with 'risk factors' that could influence or change the dynamics of their friendship. For example, if a new person were to join the group they might need to use the SC to redefine each person's role in the friendship. Likewise, if someone chose to leave the group the girls might also need the SC process and/or outside support.

Overall, Glasser's concept of the solving circle was a useful tool for facilitating relationship change. The SC prompted self-reflection and internal motivation to change within each girl and, in doing so, offered them an alternative method to solve their relationship difficulties beyond traditional external control techniques.

Relationships and conflict-solving (classroom and playground) with infants

Debbie Hoy and Ros Daniels

Debbie Hoy and Ros Daniels share how they help young children (infant age) rebuild relationships that are affected by friendship squabbles, exclusion tactics and 'bullying'.

Many of the fundamental skills of problem-solving can be introduced at infant level given planning, structure, teaching (they are skills as well as attitudes) and school-wide support.

At the time of this case example Debbie and Ros were infant teachers in a London school.

ISSUE 1 – FRIENDSHIP DIFFICULTIES

Scenario

Molly and Kyrsten (ages six and seven) were having minor conflicts with each other in class and on the playground. A wider group of friends were also being drawn into the behaviour, which was causing some of them to be excluded from the group. It began with low frequency and low intensity behaviours and grew into high frequency and high intensity behaviours bordering on intimidation and bullying (including name-calling, using unkind speech and exclusion from games).

Both sets of parents were concerned about 'bullying' and about the effect that the situations were having on the children at home as well as at school; their academic work was suffering and they were unhappy. They each made appointments to talk about the situation and I reassured them that it would be fully investigated and that I would feed back to them.

School response

My investigation included:

▶ **Talking to the class teacher**
I spoke to the class teacher about the parental concerns and asked for some background information. She was already aware of the issues and agreed that I should get involved with investigating and supporting the children.
▶ **Speaking to each of the two girls individually**
I went to the classroom and asked each child if they would be happy to have

a chat with me. I talked to each of them individually and explained that I had spoken to their parents. I asked them to tell me what was making them feel unhappy in school and they each described incidents from their own perspective. I asked open questions as appropriate and reflected back some of what I had been told to gather a wider picture. I asked them if there was anything that could help to resolve the situation and gave them some suggestions (e.g. 'Would it help if we talked to Molly?'). We agreed that it would be helpful to set up a meeting where the two girls could talk together and I would act as facilitator.

▶ **Meeting with the two girls together**
Both children were given the opportunity of telling the other how they felt about the conflict: 'Kyrsten, tell Molly how you felt when she left you out of the game'. They were then given the chance to respond. They both said sorry to each other, naming the behaviour that they were sorry for ('Sorry for not sharing our game with you') and I explained that sorry was a promise, which meant that they would try not do it again. We agreed that it would be helpful to meet with the other children and draw up some rules for the friendship group.

▶ **Meeting with the group of five girls together**
The other three children joined us in the room and we met in a circle. I explained where we had got to so far in resolving the issues and that we wanted to draw up some rules or guidelines for the friendship.

▶ **Agreeing on a list of 'friendship rules' and consequences**
We discussed what these might look like and I scribed for the group as they thought of the ideas. When they had been agreed, I wrote them out and we all signed the final copy. Each child was then given a photocopy to take away.

> 1 *We will talk kindly to each other.*
> 2 *We will be gentle towards each other.*
> 3 *We will listen to each other.*
> 4 *We will share our games with each other.*
> 5 *We can play with other children if we want to.*

We also agreed on a reporting strategy for the children if the problems continued. They were to report straight to the adult on supervision duty (in playground times) and also to me if there were any incidents. The consequence of breaking the friendship rules was that the child would lose the right to play with the group.

▶ **Feedback to parents**
Both sets of parents were informed of the actions and of the agreement that the children had made.

▶ **Monitoring**
Over the next few days, the class teacher took responsibility for monitoring the behaviour in the classroom and asking the children how their playtimes had been for them. I also saw the children regularly during the first few days and no further issues arose. We continued to review this on a weekly basis.

Outcome

Although the process was time consuming on the day, it was time well invested. The children were able to take responsibility in their relationships and had strategies for dealing with the difficulties. The alternative could have been constant interruptions after each playtime to sort out the difficulties they had been having. The parents said that the children had not had any further difficulties after the initial meetings.

ISSUE 2 – ATTITUDE PROBLEM

Scenario

Rupert (aged six) was a highly articulate, very able and self-assured child. He enjoyed school, and when motivated by the subject, was eager to learn new information. Rupert had made a positive start to the new school year and had responded well to the establishment of the shared class rules and responsibilities.

However, on occasions, he had an attitude that the learning in the classroom was 'beneath him'. At times like this it was challenging to keep him on task and he could become verbally abusive towards adults and other children. After several incidents of exhibiting this behaviour and being sent out to the parallel class, it was agreed that we would work with him on changing his behaviour with a long-term plan. We set aside a day to achieve this.

School response

The process included:

▶ **Talking to the class teacher**
I gathered a wider picture of when the incidents had happened and their frequency and intensity.
▶ **Withdrawing the child from the class**
Having been given a choice with a consequence, Rupert was withdrawn from the classroom with all of his school and personal belongings. Some of the time was used for him to catch up on his work, and the rest of the day was spent working on teaching corrective procedures.
▶ **Working with Rupert individually**
Rupert and I talked through the behaviours that he had exhibited and he was very truthful about what he had done. He felt uncomfortable outside of his classroom and wanted to know what he had to do to get back into class. We had a thoughtful discussion about the definition of being sorry and what it looks like to be sorry. We built a mind map to show the negative behaviours and how to change them into positives. Rupert had to think very hard about how he was going to change the behaviours and with support he came up with

realistic targets for change. Rupert was genuinely sorry and wrote letters to the people who had been affected by his behaviour (including his mother).

► **Reintegrating him back into the class**

Towards the end of the afternoon, Rupert was ready to return to his own class. He took all his belongings and the 'sorry' letters. The children were in a circle when he returned and were very pleased to see him. After he had given out his sorry letters, Rupert received a card of friendship from the children. This was probably the most significant factor in the whole day, as he needed the reinforcement of being accepted by his peers.

► **Monitoring**

The class teacher monitored his progress towards the behaviour targets and I also reinforced his progress throughout the day as he completed tasks.

► **Feedback to parent**

Rupert's mother was fully involved with this process and is positively rewarding his school behaviours.

Outcome

Since that day, Rupert has continued to use his positive behaviour targets and is now, himself, supporting other children.

TELLING THE TRUTH

We have found that children are more likely to tell the truth if we make it safe for them to do so. This involves the adult being calm, fair and consistent.

We usually give the child options, naming the incident, and telling them that if they do tell the truth all we will say to them is, 'Thank you for telling the truth' and then ask them to put it right and help them to put it right.

Example of options given:

► Maybe you did *punch Tom in the stomach* and you did it on purpose and now you feel sorry.
► Maybe you did *punch him* but you didn't mean to.
► Maybe you didn't *punch him* at all.

This usually results in the child taking the middle option and saying it was an accident. We thank them for being brave enough to tell the truth and talk about what they can do to put it right and resolve the situation.

A small minority will say, 'I don't know' and at that point it can help to ask them a question such as, 'If you thought you knew, what would it be?' If they still deny their involvement and you have evidence to the contrary, then allow them more thinking time. It is important to reassure the child that you are confident that they will be brave enough to be truthful and remind them that whatever they say, you will remain calm and fair and will be proud of them for being truthful even if you don't like their behaviour.

Working with children using sharing in group meetings is time consuming initially but always productive in its longer-term outcomes. Children begin to understand they have a genuine voice and an opportunity to share their feelings and concerns. They can then work towards more constructive and co-operative solutions to their problems.

What may seem small or insignificant to a teacher can loom large in the minds of children. When teachers take time, and *make time*, to listen and to guide individuals and groups in both needs-sharing and solution-oriented thinking, the results are always more rewarding for all concerned.

Editor's note: I would like to strongly recommend a read-aloud picture story book on bullying for infant and middle school primary years called *No More Bullying* by Rosemary Stones (published by Dinosaur, HarperCollins imprint.) This book is a powerful awareness-raising option and starting point for any class or small group discussion. It clearly relates to young children's experience of school and will assist both victim and bully and raise awareness of the nature of bullying and how to address it within a school.

Creating the peaceable school

Carmel Ryan

What is a peaceable school? What does it look, sound, feel like? Carmel Ryan (a deputy principal, primary) shares her thoughts. Her school has been consciously focused on developing a more 'peaceable' school through 'The Labrador Peaceable Schools Project'.

Many people seem genuinely interested in the present state of play at our school. 'How far along the journey are you now? Have you noticed any appreciable differences since you developed a focus on a "peaceable" school?' Others simply remark, 'Oh, you're the experts!' (if only, I muse …) or 'Holy cow! I read your article on "peaceable schools". That seems like an awful lot of work to improve student behaviour. What about the rest of the job?' (Pay now or pay later, I think. There is a return on the investment but on the 'pay later' plan, interest accumulates. Personal choice.)

A SNAPSHOP OF A PEACEABLE SCHOOL

And so I sit with pen poised trying to encapsulate briefly the spirit of a philosophy that is still evolving, still challenging, still frustrating but still exciting in its limitless potential.

Do I try to paint a picture of the peer support students, who, without external motivation, (no stickers, no jelly babies, no play money) head up to the planning room during lunch hours 'just to help'?

Do I explain the 'planning room'? The place where students come in a climate of mutual respect to learn about the acceptance of responsibility for their behavioural choices, and where in an atmosphere of essential oils (smells nice), affirming posters, Bach (J.S.) and bean bags, they are led through a thinking process which could be described as a 'cognitive State of Origin match' (Australian rules football). How do I describe the mediation I requested having found myself spinning on my back wheels due to a communication problem between a Year 4 student and myself. At the mediation's conclusion Sarah, a Year 7 student, asked, 'Do you think you two could ever be friends again?'

A success story

An extract from a student's journal:

> *I have been fighting and pushing people around. I have been getting sent out of the classroom and parents have been complaining about me (to the*

police). Since I have been going into the planning room, I have learnt to co-operate around the playground and in the class. I am not going to blow it.
(Year 8 student)

A challenge

Another student wrote:

I am feeling happy because my problem has been solved by Mrs _____ and Mrs _____ and me, and we agreed to co-operate.
(Year 10 student) suspended five days later

In their own words

Student alternative plans are simple but powerful:

I will only listen to those kids who tell me not to fight.
I will no longer be a victim.

THE STARTING POINT

A historical snapshot of student management at Labrador would show that the discipline was 'good'. Relationships were valued in the main, but, in the heat of myriads of daily bushfires, we sometimes would yield to the reactive model of stimulus-response.

On the door to my office are the words, 'If better is possible then good is not enough'. I began to realise that systems change when people experience personal change. As we engage in new dialogue about our shared perspective we asked new questions:

Is this going the way we want to go?
If we keep going on this way will it get better?
Could things get worse?

Those questions finally drove us to look for new solutions: good becomes better, better becomes best. One can't change one's destination overnight, but one can change the direction. That direction for us was the exploration of William Glasser's 'Choice Theory/Reality Therapy'.

As we struggle to commit to a non-coercive environment where the concepts of non-violence, compassion, trust, respect and tolerance are the pervasive themes in the interaction of student-student, student-teacher, teacher-teacher and teacher-parent, we can focus on the real business of learning. I can hear the cry, 'But you don't understand. Our problems are different.' You're right. *Your* problems *are* different. To any school experiencing student management problems, I would say that what these examples will teach you is limited. It is necessary to know *why* a practice is successful. You cannot hope simply to duplicate a practice that may work in a particular setting. However, you can implement similar principles or guidelines and then it is a matter of trial and error – 'failing one's way' to success.

Would every member of the Labrador community agree that all attitudes, behaviours and activities have significantly improved enough to state that the journey is complete? I hope not! But it is undeniable that a metamorphosis is taking place – not rapid but sure; chaotic but organised; simple but complex; controlled but flexible; moving forward and getting stuck. New growth is always accompanied by pain. Six thousand years of recorded history reads: opportunity mixed with difficulty. Your journey (if you decide to accept it) will be no different.

If you are willing to accept that such behaviour management systems are more effective than exercising forceful authority over the learners and are needed to deal with conflict in our schools, you will share similar changes in direction.

You will begin to move from external to internal control, from stimulus-response to behavioural choices, from positive reinforcement to self-evaluation, from coercive practice to collaboration. With so much more to relate I will leave Haim Ginott (1972) to conclude :

I've come to the frightening conclusion that I am the decisive element in the classroom. It's my personal approach that creates the climate. It's my daily mood that makes the weather. As a teacher, I possess tremendous power to make a child's life miserable or joyous. I can be a tool of torture or an instrument of inspiration. I can humiliate or humour, hurt or heal. In all situations, it is my response that decides whether a crisis will be escalated or de-escalated and a child humanised or dehumanised.

Good luck on *your* journey.

QUICK SCENARIO

An 11-year-old girl was sent to me because she was caught stealing pencils from a classmate's tidy tray. The teacher became frustrated because the child would not admit that she had stolen the pencils. After a lunch hour of discussion and tears and denial from the 'accused' (despite the accounts of at least three witnesses), I decided to continue the conversation in the privacy of my office. At the end of about 20 minutes, I sent the child back to the classroom.

The teacher rang through to thank me for finally getting the child to admit the theft. When I replied 'But I didn't,' the teachers were perplexed. 'But everything is fine. The two students are happy. There are no tears. Life is back to normal in our classroom. What did you do?'

I related the conversation I had with the 'thief'. Forcing myself to take a completely different tack (I felt sure she was guilty as well), I asked Jane, 'What do you want?' She replied, 'I just want someone to believe me.'

'Okay, despite the mounting evidence Jane, I believe you. But we still have a problem, don't we? What is it?'

'Well, Jackie doesn't have her pencils and the kids and teachers all hate me for all the fuss and my lying.'

'Okay, is there any way to make it right?'

'Well, I could give Jackie all the pencils I have in my bag and say I'm sorry for all the fuss.'

'Why don't you do that and come back and see me.'

About ten minutes later both students returned smiling and happy. Jackie was more than happy with the pencils and the apology. Jane returned to the classroom and Jackie asked to see me privately. She said, 'I really still believe Jane took my pencils, but she is pretty poor and I think I know how she felt with everyone coming down on her. I think she's learnt a lot from this and she'll think twice before she does something like this again.'

We had a win-win situation. I could have been unyielding, humiliating Jane into admitting the theft. What would have been achieved? Some people who are into 'boss' management and punishment would call the outcome 'weak', with Jane getting away with it.

Weeks later the students are still friends, the teacher reports no animosity, the 'thief' comes regularly to the planning room to help other students. We all know the truth, but the reality has more substance. The student still has her self-respect, relationships are being enhanced. Haven't we all made mistakes now and then?

People or events outside us never merely stimulate us to do anything. In this case we all followed the rules of the game to achieve the most meaningful outcome for us all – respect and value for the individual no matter what the choice.

A beautiful place: building a multicultural school

Larry Schwartz

In Noble Park Secondary College, children and teachers from around the world are building a harmonious, multicultural school that may be a pointer to Australia's future. Larry Schwartz reports. Peter D'Angelo shares how teachers can build confidence in their students and a positive sense of community – even in a busy classroom context.

Larry is a reporter with The Age newspaper, Melbourne.

Early afternoon in classroom B8. Tiny fish flit about a small aquarium. A blue-tongued lizard among lifeless specimens preserved in jars. 'You get a release?' asks the teacher. 'Of insulin,' says one of 17 students in this afternoon's Year 12 biology class. 'Diana, can you read that please?' says the teacher. 'Michael, have you done question three?' 'You all right, Scott?'

Nives takes notes diligently. Once she sat in a class in Trebinje, in her native Bosnia-Herzegovina. Then came a war.

'The bombing was probably the main thing,' she says. 'When you're seven years old, you don't expect that to happen in your own secure world.'

Nives' parents came from Dubrovnik, in Croatia. Among her closest friends, classmate Jenita is from Bosnia and Adriana is from Serbia.

'You don't look at the person for the background,' Nives says. 'You look at them as a person. We probably sometimes discuss the issues because being in a war is not exactly what everyone experiences or everyone would like to experience. (But) it's not a very big topic between us. We just talk about normal teenage things.'

Noble Park Secondary College is among Australia's most ethnically diverse schools. Almost half the 708 students were born overseas. Just three in 10 have an English-speaking background. At home, many will slip into one of more than 50 languages and dialects. They have come with their families from around the globe: Afghanistan, Croatia, East Timor, Cambodia, Thailand, Turkey, India, Chile, Ethiopia, Hong Kong, Western Samoa and more. Yet proudly displayed on a corridor wall is the Australian citizenship pledge.

Nives reads and write poetry – Keats 'Ode to a Nightingale' is her favourite – but she hopes to study medicine or law.

Her family spent two years in a Danish town, Grena, before settling here in 1994. When Nives came here, she could speak several languages from the former Yugoslavia as well as Danish, Swedish and Norwegian. But she knew just one word in English.

'I think from cartoon the only word I knew was "dog",' says the 17-year-old, who learnt the language in a month of watching TV and reading newspapers. 'It's very weird.'

Created from the merger in 1994 of Noble Park Heights Secondary College and Noble Secondary College, the school is accessible through a side street, secluded from the hubbub of south-eastern suburbia by sporting fields and gums. Some of the factories that lured the rich mix of migrants have closed in recent years. Yet there is a buoyancy here, a sense that there are no limits in Australia.

'Really in this country you can do whatever you like,' says Jenita, 16, a Muslim born in Sarajevo whose family lived in Berlin for three years before coming here in 1995. 'No matter if you live in Noble Park or Toorak, you can do it. That's the kind of society it is.'

A classmate, Francesca, 17, was four when her family arrived here from turmoil in Romania. 'Whatever was back in our countries was back in our countries,' says Francesca, who joined the Army Reserve last year. 'We're in Australia now. We're friends. We don't look for where we come from.'

A visitor may wonder at this harmony in diversity, but it seems natural to Richard, 18, of Anglo-Australian descent, who stacks shelves at a supermarket before school, sells second-hand mobile phones afterwards, has his own band and plans to be a sound technician.

'Being Australian,' he says, 'I've always felt safe here and when other people come I feel no resentment. I welcome them because it's ... giving Australia more diversity.'

You wonder, too, about the changing nature of Australia's identity. 'The rate of change is still too fast to freeze in an identity,' says Bill, 17, who isn't sure when his British forebears came to Australia. 'The rate of change has to slow down to get a real identity.'

The friendship between Nives, Jenita and Adriana has impressed their English teacher, Peter D'Angelo (see Chapter 1, p 12) To him, the bond epitomises how national tensions can be transcended.

'You'd think there'd be racism but there isn't,' he says of the school. D'Angelo taught some of the students here when they were newly arrived refugees, at nearby Noble Park English Language School, one of four Melbourne schools for migrants and refugees. He is now integration co-ordinator and one of nine teachers of English as a second language at Noble Park Secondary. He is also a poet and author who has written extensively on the migrant experience.

Now 47, he was four-and-a-half when his family migrated from Italy's Abruzzi region. His maternal grandfather had a gift for him as he prepared to embark on a converted cargo vessel, the *Oceania*, with his mother and two sisters for a 31-day trip to a faraway land where he would meet his father, who had gone on ahead before he was born. 'My grandfather gave me a pair of sunglasses – and I know this sounds corny but it did happen – and he said: "Put these on when you reach Australia and you'll see a beautiful place".'

His grandfather had told him, too, to use the sunglasses to look out for dolphins. Once he did. But the glasses were broken by a boy on board. There was a borrowed grey car to collect them from Station Pier. The house his father had set out to build was not complete. The family slept on a concrete floor.

In the title poem of his collection *Folk Songs*, he writes of migrants hurried down gangways to shouts of 'bloody refos!', hard times on production lines. And domestic discord with a widening gap between generations.

We sent our children to school but they came home with more than English; strange tongues crept into kitchens, began questioning customs, then dividing our lives ...

It's an experience familiar to Yoko, 17. 'I think there is a gap because my parents are from Japan and they still have that Japanese culture,' she says. 'They don't get as much exposed to Australia as I do because I go to school. I meet all these people and they're from different cultures. I think everyone gets more exposed to Australia than their parents do.'

D'Angelo has watched some students progress from their first months in Australia. Lino, 18, was 12 when he arrived from East Timor. D'Angelo says Lino has grown in confidence but the bright smile was there from the start. Lino plans to learn carpentry before returning to Dili to help rebuild his country.

'I would rather go back,' he says. 'I've got more relatives there. When I go back I can find a job easier because the war isn't happening.'

Nives has already been back to her birthplace. 'At the beginning I didn't feel like going much,' she says. 'I wanted to see my family and all but I didn't think I wanted to go back to that place because obviously the memories were a bit mixed. So I was overwhelmed when I went over there. I absolutely loved it.'

'But even though it was a great experience, it was very hard for me. I think I still call Australia home, as clichéd as that sounds. I was happy to come back here.'

We meet again in a conference room. Of four students attending a Student Representative Council meeting, one was born in Australia. The others came from Romania, Afghanistan and New Zealand.

'I knew how to spell my name, that's all,' says quietly spoken Farooq, 14, recalling when his family fled Kabul four years ago. 'We just wanted to stay there but we couldn't because there was killing and everything. We had to leave our house behind us ... We just wanted peace.'

His mother worries that her three sons might marry outside the Muslim faith. 'Most parents want their kids to be in their religion,' he says, 'and they want them to be strict. But they just can't because they drift away with others at school and everything.'

Farooq has a passion for Australian rules football. Last year he won a best and fairest vote in the Dandenong district league. His family lived in Sydney before coming to Melbourne, so he barracks for the Swans (a famous Australian football team). He first played in the under-11s for a local club and still cringes at an early mistake.

'I remember I handballed through the goals. I thought there was going to be a goal. I remember that. I grabbed the ball and the goals were in front of me. I thought "easy goal", I just handballed it through. It was quite embarrassing ...'

Demons skipper David Neitz, *Kangaroo* Glenn Archer and *Collingwood's* late Darren Millane came from the same club.

Farooq dreams of one day playing for the *Swans*. 'My mum wants me to quit. She goes, "You're going to hurt yourself." I have to go in my bedroom and watch telly when the footy is on. The whole family just hates it totally. Probably one day I'll hopefully get into the AFL (Australian Football League) and my mum can see me on the telly or something. Then she'll realise that I did it.'

Peter D'Angelo knows the trauma some have endured. 'Any sudden noises from a car exhaust, they'd flinch,' he says.

D'Angelo was inexperienced and the language school poorly equipped when he faced the disconcerting silence of Vietnamese and Cambodian children in the early 1980s. It took a while before he heard stories of rape by Thai pirates and other horrors. A Cambodian wrote a poem that perplexed him. She explained that it described how her father's face had been hacked away to reveal the white skull beneath.

The Romanians came with their stories of brutalities. Latin Americans too. 'The talk of what happened in El Salvador is also frightening,' he says. The Afghanis, fleeing Soviet invasion. Bosnians in the early 1990s. Again and again he told himself, 'It just can't get any worse than this.' *Teaching was so much more than a job.* 'I realised that I had to give them the best I could because it wasn't a job anymore. It was a … true vocation.'

But his approach demanded so much that he came to withdraw and, for a while, tried not to give so much of himself. A 16-year-old Bosnian girl he taught had a spirited good nature and ready smile despite kidney and liver disease, loss of sight in one eye and post-trauma epileptic fits. Her father had been beaten and taken away. She and her mother were raped by soldiers. One day, she showed him some lines she had written:

I am the essence of my people
And the spirit of my past,
In this new land
I will take as always
The good and the bad …

Her example inspired him. 'I was teaching kids to write poetry in a very detached way,' he says. 'It clicked that I was doing it without the real feeling there. I think she clicked too. She wrote a poem and thanked me for teaching her English so she could write about her feelings.'

'Here I was, doing it by rote. I was cheating my students. I was becoming like a zombie. She made me come back. That's when I decided to extend it. I wanted to see these kids in another context, which was this school here.'

D'Angelo initiated our visit to the school and organised a discussion between more than 20 students. Such was the diversity, it seemed this might be emblematic of a future Australia. He believes Australia is more confident and tolerant than when he came here as a child.

'I feel it's at a stage where it needs to take a final step and we can be anything we want to be. I think these kids have got it in their power to do that.'

A *human story*

A colleague of mine found this on the Internet (unsourced).
I do not doubt its veracity – or its universal message.

A few years ago at the Special Olympics held in Seattle in the United States, nine contestants, all physically or mentally disabled, assembled at the starting line for the 100 yard dash. At the sound of the gun, they all started out, not exactly in a dash, but with a relish to run the race to the finish and win.

All, that is, except for one boy who stumbled on the asphalt, tumbled over a couple of times, and began to cry. The other eight heard the boy cry. They slowed down and paused. Then they all turned around and went back. Every one of them. One girl with Down's syndrome bent down and kissed him and said, 'This will make it better'. Then all nine linked arms and walked together to the finishing line.

Everyone in the stadium stood and the cheering went on for ten minutes. People who were there are still telling the story. Why? … Because deep down we know this one thing: What matters in life is more than winning for yourself. What truly matters in this life is helping others win, even if it means slowing yourself down and changing your course.

6

Essential Principles and Practices that Enable Us to Make a Difference with Individual Children and Classroom Groups

We learn from each other as teachers. We teach each other; by default or design.

Entering into a colleague's classroom – even in print – can provide a shared collegial awareness of our common task, our common struggle. It can also remind us how we find the energy, goodwill and support to build the kind of relationships that effect the sorts of changes these stories detail.

These are children and young people whose thinking attitude, self-esteem and learning have been directly affected by the colleagues we read about here. There are common themes, understanding, skills and teacher behaviours that clearly brought about those 'differences' in affect and behaviour.

While there is obvious variance among schools in terms of school populations, local areas, teaching styles, leadership styles, policies, the physical resources in a school and the quality of its colleague culture (in terms of support and teamwork) – common understandings, principles and practices clearly emerge across all these teachers.

COLLEAGUE SUPPORT

In each account in this book teachers note the crucial nature of colleague support.

Moral support

This is the no-blame attitude that shares the 'common lot'; that colleague watchfulness where we consciously look out for one another, particularly in times of crisis (as when a student is 'holding a class to ransom'). Teachers are not blamed when asking for help – help is offered early, before things get too out of hand.

In some schools there is that tension between a teacher needing and wanting support (sometimes desperately) and the anxiety that if they do ask they will be perceived as inadequate, ineffective, or – worse – incompetent. The issue of a teacher's competency is, of course, a significant factor that sometimes needs to be painfully addressed. However, a school should distinguish between long-term professional 'performance' concerns and the need to offer *early* and *strategic colleague support* to a colleague who is clearly struggling with a challenging child or class.

There is wide research that demonstrates a significant correlation between teacher stress, coping, welfare and teacher effectiveness (in change of practice) on the one hand and the quality and extent of on-going colleague support offered in a given school (Rogers, 2002a). In the schools we read about here, colleague support is offered early; without censure or implied 'blame' and clearly with a sense of shared struggle.

Structural support

Changes began to occur when some structure or plan changed the focus of teacher and students' attention from the natural stress of whatever is occurring to the possibilities of seeing things, and doing things, differently. Each teacher finds some 'plan', 'key' or 'process' within which to support an individual or class group. This always arises out of a genuine desire to 'connect' and engage with the student and then to support the student to gain awareness of their behaviour and effect change.

The common forms of support noted by colleagues are:

▶ A behaviour, welfare and discipline policy with a clear focus on positive discipline practices (rather than reactive, *ad hoc* practice). Such a policy has due behaviour consequences based on the principle of 'negotiated' options (including mediation, restitution and even classroom meetings) as well as non-negotiable consequences for serious behaviours such as violence, bullying, drugs and weapons.
▶ Adequate, and school-wide, time-out options for repeatedly distracting and disruptive students.
▶ Seeking to keep the focus of the consequences on the *fair certainty* of due process rather than 'severity'. Teachers do not use a behaviour consequence (such as follow-up beyond the classroom, detention or withdrawal of privileges) as an opportunity to berate the student or engage in some kind of 'emotional pay-back' (tempting as that might be). Further, they always emphasise the need to repair and rebuild with the child and to help the child repair and rebuild with their peers. While this is a labour-intensive aspect of our teacher leadership it goes a long way to achieving a more positive and peaceable school.

Chapter 3 outlines a common 'structure' or form of support that of helping a teacher develop individual behaviour management plans with children with repeatedly attentional, distracting, disruptive or emotionally disordered behaviours. The concept of individual behaviour management plans is widely and commonly used in supportive schools. While their main emphasis is to give the child behaviour and learning skills they also give individual teachers a structure within which to change their teaching focus and support with the child.

Professional support

Each teacher (in this book) values the insight, problem-sharing, analysis and shared action-planning offered by their colleagues. Sometimes this involves team meetings and the on-going reassurance that we're 'on the right track', at other times it involves mentoring with a colleague in the classroom to work with an individual child, to help conduct a classroom meeting or to help a colleague develop a 'fresh start' process with a challenging classroom group (see Chapter 4).

One colleague writes about how colleague support helped rebuild her confidence in the utility and benefits of classroom meetings.

> *When I conducted my first classroom meeting with a composite grade 5/6 they were a very difficult class and I was hoping to use the meeting format to readdress where we were going as a class – to move towards a 'fresh start'.*
>
> *The meeting was loud – raucous in fact. Frequent calling out and 'Shut up!! I'm talking ...' There were put downs ('Stupid' 'Won't work!') when solutions were proposed. I stopped the meeting after 20 minutes! I changed the activity to the class now writing an evaluation of their behaviour at the meeting. It helped regain some sanity.*
>
> *I shared what I'd gone through with colleagues and got* immediate *support. A colleague and I discussed what had happened and they came into class with me to help me conduct the next classroom meeting; we had a separate place for the classroom meeting (not the classroom); used name cards (to be turned over when anyone in the group wished to speak or contribute); had a set routine for listing, discussing and offering solutions to problems choosing workable solutions and having a time limit for the classroom meeting.* (See Rogers, 1992, p54).

Anne notes that it was the presence (and good humour) of her colleague – with her in the room – (and discussing and sharing before and after) that made the difference to the on-going success of classroom meetings.

WHOLE-SCHOOL EMPHASIS

In many of the schools the individual teacher's struggle with a challenging student or class is an issue addressed on a whole-school basis. Teachers are not left in moral, 'structural' or professional isolation. As one teacher said to me recently, 'In our school a "problem-child" is not just *your* problem it is *our* problem ... If an incident has occurred with a grade teacher's child on playground duty nobody goes up to that teacher and says, "Do you know what your Johnny or Tracey did in the playground?". When a child's behaviour is an issue in the playground that child is everyone's child not just the grade teacher's child.'

Whenever a child's behaviour is *frequent, general* and *durable* (more than bad-day syndrome) then the individual teacher has support (from their colleagues) to develop an individual behaviour management plan with the child. Such plans (see Chapter 3) often give the student the structure they need within which to learn and supportively develop new skills for behaviour and formal learning.

The whole-school emphasis also includes well developed time-out options (noted earlier) and mediation and restitutional opportunities.

As in all colleague support, *form follows function*. The *function* of colleague support is to meet teachers' needs (their espoused, not *assumed*, need). In consciously supportive cultures, senior staff engage that process of espoused needs-analysis on a regular basis and work with staff to provide dependable *forms* of colleague support (structures, plans, policies, professional teaming options – formal and informal). When teachers believe their needs are being heard, engaged with and realistically addressed they feel better and take on their professional role with more confidence and goodwill (Rogers, 2002b).

THE ON-GOING WILLINGNESS TO PERSIST, COUPLED WITH AN UNFLAGGING RESPECT FOR THE CHILD

Children who frequently display attentional and challenging behaviours in classrooms and playgrounds are not easy to 'like'. Liking a student is not something we can easily manufacture – dependent as it is on mood, circumstance, weather, available time … Respecting the essential person is no mean feat when they are driving you 'round the twist' or 'up the wall'. These teachers have managed to gain a perspective – within their stressful circumstances – so that they have learned to see the white square as much bigger than the darkish dot in the centre (see the diagram overleaf). It is easy, so easy, to *just* focus on the dot at the expense of the space in the rest of the square. I've used this metaphor with students. Initially all they can see is the dot when asked, 'What can you see here?' When asked different questions they eventually see that almost all of the square is the 'space'. The metaphor is developed as the space representing what is better, more helpful, positive, less stressful, more realistically possible in contrast to the 'dark dot' – the stressful or difficult aspect of life at the moment. I've also used this visual metaphor with colleagues and some have said, 'The dark dot is too big!'. Our collegial response is, 'How can we make the white space bigger?' The 'white space' is the colleague support offered in good faith, giving whatever we can to manage the 'dark dot' as it were.

These teachers *persist* with the child, with the class. That persistence is based in a communicated respect for the individual coupled with a belief that things *can be different*.

This persistence and belief is given psychological and relational 'flesh' through structures and programmes, but in the end it is the teacher's belief in the child, and the group, that comes through to make the difference.

When children's behaviour is rude (and crude), lazy, arrogant, selfish and insensitive it is not easy to keep the focus on the fundamental person; and how we can discipline *and support*, with some dignity. These children chip away at our natural and professional goodwill. If we choose to work with challenging children it is, naturally, stressful and there is a frustrating 'normality' about this stressful reality. That stress is better managed, and our coping resources far more effectively engaged, when we have on-going colleague support. It helps when we know that we're all 'in the same boat' – a little leaky at times, perhaps a bit rusty, but be assured the boat is still viable, working, the rudder and compass OK …

and we're 'getting around those icebergs' (as one colleague deftly put it) 'so we're *still* stressed but not *as* stressed, *as* often, *as* long … (Rogers, 2002b).

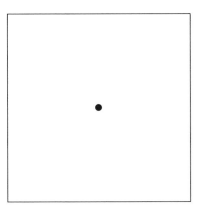

THE 'BAD-DAY SYNDROME'

These teachers also acknowledge that within their naturally stressful role they do have bad days when they 'snap' at students, say the 'wrong thing' (to a student or class) or forget to encourage (when it would have really helped…). Teachers can be incredibly hard on themselves, not least when they start comparing themselves to teachers they believe (or perceive) are more successful with challenging students (or groups).

ACCEPTING FALLIBILITY IN OURSELVES AND IN OTHERS

All humans are fallible. We recognise that we fail (we are not *failures*); we forget; we make stupid mistakes and, of course, we get tired and fed-up – and why wouldn't we? Mentally kicking oneself ('I *should have* done this … or that … I *never* get it right …', 'I'll *never* get through to that kid … that class') is understandable, but detrimental. If our characteristic explanatory style for stressful events is to 'globalise' – 'all', 'never', 'no one', e.g. '*All* the kids in my class are animals!' not only will that add to our stress it will significantly affect our coping ability and our ability to focus on, and orient, change. (Rogers, 1996 and 2002b).

There is a big difference, however, between accepting fallibility and unwillingness to address what we know is repeatedly, and *characteristically*, working against our shared aims and shared practices as a collegial team.

SEPARATING THE BEHAVIOUR FROM THE PERSON

This is a message as old as the human family. Whenever an adult is in a role of leadership with others they have to learn to see the person beyond the inappropriate or wrong behaviour while at the same time not excusing the inappropriate or wrong behaviour.

This asks a lot of us as teachers – yet the teachers writing here respond to that call. They see the white space as well as the 'dot', while not allowing the dot to take 'centre stage' (p 101).

They also do not 'revictimise' the child because of his family background or where he comes from. They recognise that while we clearly cannot control the many factors affecting a child's attitude and behaviour these teachers believe they can help the child to believe in themselves and bring about positive change in behaviour and learning *while at school*.

FOCUSING ON THE CHILD'S EFFORT TOWARDS CHANGE

Merely telling the child they should (or should not) behave in this way will rarely bring about change. Worse, simply telling them louder, or longer, will often reinforce attentional or power-seeking patterns of behaviour. Unless a child sees a need to change, has a reason for change, and is given motivation, on-going support, hope and, often, a 'plan' for change, they may resist what we believe are our good motives in our discipline.

Of course children need discipline but discipline is never an end in itself; it is always a means to an end.

Children need, and want, to 'belong'. It is a primary social need (Adler, 1957; Dreikers et al, 1982; Erickson, 1968; Glasser,1986; Coopersmith, 1967; Maslow, 1970). *Some* children feel and believe (with relative degrees of consciousness) that they can only really belong when they are drawing significant attention to themselves, or engaging their teachers in power struggles. Teachers variously describe these children as significantly attention-seeking or power-seeking. Their behaviour is – in effect – their goal; seeking to belong. This 'goal', while appearing negative to many teachers, does self-confirm in many children in that they often achieve the 'goal' they seek: the attention or power. The 'private logic' of the child confirms the belief of significance gained by behaviour (even negative behaviour) (Dreikurs et al, 1982).

Even when we *overly* attend, nag, engage or threaten students who repeatedly call out, clown around, answer back or challenge we re-confirm in these children their goals of attention or power.

It is not easy to *consciously* step back and ask ourselves (in the less stressful moment): how can I re-engage this child so I can give them the beneficial help they need? How can I reframe – positively – the sense of personal power that will strengthen their self-concept? These teachers have managed to do that. To balance appropriate discipline with not reinforcing the child's mistaken goals.

Supportive interventions in schools help the child in their need to belong, giving them hope in the purpose and direction of behaviour change. When children (indeed adults) feel, believe and behave as if they have meaningful control over their lives they feel, and do, better. Even when we need to discipline we can do so in ways that keep the fundamental dignity of the child intact while still addressing the inappropriate, disruptive or even dysfunctional behaviour.

FOCUSING ON THE 'PRIMARY' BEHAVIOUR OR ISSUE

When children 'sneer', 'pout', 'sulk', 'sigh', 'raise their eyes to the ceiling' and display other such irritating non-verbal behaviours these teachers consciously seek to keep the focus of their discipline engagement on the primary issue or behaviour, rather than focus on the 'secondary' issues. This is a daily (hourly) challenge for teachers in the 'emotional moment' when a child responds to a teacher's reminder, direction or question in a 'sulky', 'pouty', 'sighing' manner. When the student looks like you've asked them to fly to the moon because you've asked them to 'put up your hand', 'wait your turn', 'go back to your seat', 'carry on with your work', 'remember our rule for …' – it is not easy to keep the focus of our discipline on the *main* or *primary issue* at that moment when emotions are naturally raised:

> *I was working with a challenging class in Western Sydney a few years back. As soon as the noisy, restless students came into the classroom (including a couple of lads 'testosteronically bonding' – 'We're just mucking around!'), three girls raced to the back of the room and began to loudly rearrange the last row of tables and chairs – moving them to the far, back, right corner of the classroom (I suspected to create a small 'bloc').*
>
> *Instead of formally beginning the lesson (from the front of the classroom) I walked over to the girls (the rest of the class sensing, watching …). The girls were sitting in their chairs but had pushed their tables right away from all the others to the far back corner of the room. It was my first meeting with this class so I asked them for their names. 'What's your name please?' I believe I was pleasant as I made eye-contact with the first student. She leaned back in her chair, raised her eyes, sighed and said, 'What do you want to know my name for?' Her barely controlled insolence, her tone, her manner needed to be addressed without getting into unnecessary confrontation. I also wanted to keep the focus on the main or primary issue of moving the furniture – now added to by the tone and manner of her response. I also wanted to do this as quickly as possible, realising the potential audience-seeking capacity (perhaps habituated?) of this student.*
>
> *'I'm not speaking rudely to you, I don't expect you to speak rudely to me.' I kept eye-contact, but also looked at the other girls (might they collude with her?). The Year 8 student leaned back: 'Rude?! What's rude!?'*
>
> *I added, 'I'm not speaking rudely or defensively to you, I don't expect you to speak that way to me.' In this very brief exchange (it nearly always seems longer in the immediate, emotional moment) I was conscious of speaking calmly but with* relaxed *assertion. (Open body language and* not *conveying a threat – I'm facing a 14-year-old girl. She's not my enemy, she's a student.)*
>
> *I repeated the first question: 'What's your name please? I'm one of the new teachers here.' 'Talia.' – it came out as a sigh, with raised eyes, folded arms; these are 'secondary behaviours'. We can learn to tactically ignore, in the emotional moment and keep the focus on the main or 'primary' issue. 'Talia, Sophie and Hailey,' (the other two girls were*

co-operative in response, in manner), 'you've rearranged the furniture – it belongs back there.' I pointed back behind me.

In this exchange I was also aware that the whole class was watching this interaction – why wouldn't they? I was also aware that the young girl's behaviour (the attentionally challenging behaviour) was, no doubt, seeking peer-audience. I was conscious of seeking to lead this situation so that the audience (of peers) would more likely accept the necessary teacher leadership, thus minimising the student's attentional goal. This, of course, is never easy in the emotional moment.

In response to the incidental direction to put the chairs back to the 'normal place' Talia leaned back with a hurt scowl: 'But we're only sitting here 'cos we're friends!' (It's tempting to retort, 'Who'd be friend to you!') A bit of partial agreement, *however, goes a long way. 'I have no problems with you sitting together as friends. However, the furniture belongs back there. That's where I expect it to go. Thank you.' At that point it helps to give 'take-up time' by 'disengaging' and physically moving away – while conveying expectation of co-operation, commonsense or (at least) compliance (Rogers, 1998).*

As I turned and moved away I could 'see' them move the furniture back, Talia muttering, sighing, 'Gees, new teacher, new teacher ... na, na, na ...' (at just above sotto voce). *Again, it is this sort of 'secondary behaviour' we* tactically ignore, *keeping the focus on the main ('primary') issue at that point: the furniture going back (and having addressed the initial rudeness). Aspects of 'secondary behaviour' such as* attitude *expressed in sighs, raised eyes, muttered whingeing (unless overtly rude or unsafe) can often be addressed later – away from the audience – (Rogers, 1998) by follow-up with the student in a calmer moment.*

At that point I went back to the front of the class and formally started yet another lesson (albeit with a new and challenging class).

NB: If Talia had refused to move (as I requested) I would have given a deferred consequence. *'Talia, if you choose not to move the furniture back now, I'll have to follow this up at recess.' At that point it's helpful to give the student take-up time. If the student mutters, 'Don't care', a brief, 'I do' (and take-up time) is enough. It will be essential, though, to follow up later with fair certainty. What is important, in such cases, is to put the responsibility back onto the student (particularly at adolescent level).*

It sounds as if this approach is time-consuming. It is actually less time-consuming, both in the immediate emotional moment and in the necessary follow-up with the student (one-to-one) later, away from their peer audience.

It is important to avoid using interrogatives in discipline situations, e.g. **'Why** did you move the furniture?' or 'You shouldn't have moved it, **should you?'** or the really unhelpful interrogative **'Have you** moved the furniture?' It is enough to describe the **obvious reality.** 'You've moved... they belong there...' (This acts as an 'incidental direction'.)

DISCIPLINE

My colleagues and I have learned that when we need to discipline our students we seek to follow these guidelines:

▶ Avoid *unnecessary* **confrontation** (most of the time).
▶ Keep the **intervention** *non-intrusive* where possible, or if we need to become *more intrusive* that does not equate to becoming more hostile or verbally aggressive – it will mean becoming more assertive. Assertion is a skill, it can be learned.
▶ Keep the **corrective language positive** (where possible).
▶ Keep the corrective discipline **focused on the 'primary' issue or behaviour** and avoid getting caught up in 'secondary' issues or behaviours such as those noted earlier or the standard 'But other teachers let us sit where we want', 'listen to Walkmans', 'chew gum', 'wear hats in class', 'dance on the tables in an east wind …'). The answer here is 'I don't know what other teachers do, in our class we …' or ' … the school rule is …'. It is important not to get into arguments about which teachers let students sit where they want, etc. It is important to refocus the student by question or rule-reminder back to the fair school rule.
▶ Keep the fundamental **respect** for the student – as a person – intact. *Always* easier said than done.
▶ **Follow up** all repeatedly distracting or disruptive behaviour on a one-to-one basis after class, or some time later that day. This says 'I care', 'It's important', 'We need to think about behaviour now and for the next time we're together in class …' It also demonstrates the **fair certainty of appropriate consequences**. Use such time to **repair and rebuild**. Even a few brief words and 'separating amicably' can enhance repairing and rebuilding, where distracting and disruptive behaviours are on-going. It is crucial to seek colleague support and pursue individual behaviour management plans (behaviour recovery) (see Chapter 3).
▶ **Distinguish between 'negotiable' and 'non-negotiable' consequences.** Non-negotiable consequences are those we apply for any *repeatedly* disturbing or unsafe behaviour, or for any aggressive, hostile or bullying behaviour, or for use of violence, intimidation, drugs or weapons.
▶ When applying consequences, **emphasise the certainty** of the consequences rather than the severity of the consequences. Also remember to keep the fundamental respect intact when *applying* the consequences.

When establishing behaviour consequences try to **establish a relationship between the disruptive behaviour and the outcome**; where appropriate ask the student what they think they should do to address the behaviour in question. Key questions that can be asked (or responded to in a standard response sheet) are:

What happened – i.e. your behaviour? (to cause you to be in detention time);
What rule (older children: *What right/rule*) *was broken?*
What's your side of it all? (right of reply)
What can you do to fix things up, make things better?
How can I help? (the initiating teacher)

This is what is meant by 'negotiable' consequences.

At the school-wide level you need to establish **degrees of seriousness** with respect to behaviour consequences (especially detention practices). Some teachers will use inappropriate detentions (even formal detentions) for behaviours that are more effectively addressed by a personal one-to-one talk with the student. It is always worth a school reviewing its detention policy to address what behaviours lead to formal detention and internal or external temporary exclusion from classes.

▶ **Establish year level and school-wide processes for exit, time-out and follow-up** of any students whose disruptive behaviour has necessitated 'exit' from the classroom (safety concerns; *persistent* refusal to work within the fair rules and within reasonable teacher direction; verbal abuse). Key questions to be addressed in such a policy are: *How* do we remove the student from the class? To whom and where? How long should the student stay in time-out? What happens when students refuse to leave the classroom? What happens with the student *during* time-out? On what basis do students renegotiate entry back into the classroom? Class/subject teachers should be responsible for follow-up of time-out procedures with support of peers.

▶ **Remember the importance of re-establishing working relationships and reconciliation** between teacher and student(s) (avoid holding grudges). Where the relational issues are serious, employ supporting mediation (from colleagues) for problem-solving and resolution.

THE POWER OF LEADERSHIP – USING OUR POWER FOR, AND WITH, OUR CHILDREN

When we are engaged in the disciplining aspect of our role as teachers it can be easy to fall into the assumption that we can control others; that we can make others do what we want. Power and authority in our leadership means more than 'controlling power' – our ability to 'control' others. When working with very challenging children the exercise of power – as control and force – without responsive moral authority leads only to reactive confrontation and relational resentment. Moral authority superintends 'role' authority. The power associated with one's role authority (as teacher) needs to be understood as more than power *over* others – it is more to be considered as the power we use (as adults) *for* and *with* our students. Our aim, within such *relational power*, is to use our 'power' to motivate, engage, assist, teach and encourage our students to control their own behaviour. Even in situations where we have to physically restrain a child who is a significant danger to himself or others we consciously seek to use our power to enable the student to 'calm' himself, regain self-control and work to repair and rebuild (Rogers, 2003; O'Brien, 1998). In each of the stories in this book teachers share how they began to understand and use this *kind* of power.

To use a deceptively basic example here: I've worked with some teachers who will snatch a toy, comic, Walkman or mobile phone off a student's desk. It is annoying when students 'secrete' such items on their desk (particularly during whole-class teaching time).

Some teachers will control the event, and the student's behaviour, by simply taking the object. In 'challenging schools' taking, or forcing a student to hand over, a Walkman or mobile phone is a recipe for conflict. I've seen students quickly exited from a classroom over such pointless power exchanges.

(Teacher)	'Right, give it to me!'
(Student)	'No way – I'll put it away if it's such a big deal!'
(Teacher)	'No you won't – you'll give it to me *now*!'
(Student)	'No – no way – it's my Walkman …'
(Teacher)	'Right – if you don't hand it over you can get out of my class now.'

Student walks out, banging his chair, adding, 'It's a sh-t class anyway …!' and (of course) drawing major peer attentional significance (at least in their 'private logic'). Who won? Why was it *defined* as a conflict, as something that has to be 'won'? Does the issue have to be defined in this way – contestably?

Other teachers will use their 'power' to control *the situation* rather than the student, using their 'power' to work with the student.

A teacher notices the Walkman on the student's table and comes across to the student.

(Teacher)	'You've got your Walkman here.' (Brief 'description of reality'.)
(Student)	Student frowns, 'Yeah,' adding, 'other teachers don't say anything, as long as we get our work done.'
(Teacher)	'Maybe they don't' (brief partial agreement) 'What's the school rule about Walkmans, Travis?'
(Student)	'I told you – other teachers let us.'
(Teacher)	'You did.' (*brief* partial agreement) 'You know the school rule …' (reminder) 'I want you to put the Walkman in your bag or on my table, ta.' (a simple choice)

At this point the teacher walks away, giving 'the control' back to the student; giving the student some 'take-up time' and disengaging any potential power struggle. She realises, of course, she cannot simply make him hand over the object, or put it away. By giving a directed 'choice' (within the fair, known rules), she has put the responsibility back where it belongs – with the student. If he refuses ('chooses') not to put it away (he'll hardly put it on the teacher's desk) the teacher will go back – a little later – and give the student a deferred consequence (i.e. following up later, after class or at break – away from 'the audience of peers'). 'If you choose not to put the Walkman away, I'll have to follow this up with you after class.'

Most students do put their 'trinkets' away, with muttered sighs and whinges (which we'll *tactically ignore*). It will then be important to briefly acknowledge this and *resume task focus*: 'How's your work going? Glad to see the Walkman is away for now (wink) – let's have a look at your maths, Travis …'

When the student puts an object away they are – in effect – (at that point) granting the teacher the authority that the teacher exercises *at that point*. The teacher's tone, manner, respect, confidence and emotional intelligence all play their part naturally. This is the creative tension of teacher authority: that our *relational* power is seen in the reciprocity of characteristic student responses. As such, our power to lead comes not merely from assumptive role power ('I am a teacher therefore students *should* do what I say') but from *earning* such authority by the nature of our leadership, how we *characteristically* communicate the shared rights, responsibilities and rules that assist the relatively smooth running of a busy classroom, and engage our students through our teaching.

Is such a leadership style more than personality? Is the ability to relate well (with some success) to young people something one just *has* or can it be learned? One of the terms used for the social, relational dexterity and intuitiveness that characterises such relational leadership is 'emotional intelligence'. While some teachers do seem to have an innate sense of how to tune in, look for and sense others' needs and feelings and respond with some 'connective awareness', it is my view that any of us can learn to develop the sorts of attributions, understandings and skills that these teachers clearly exhibit. *The ability to teach and lead effectively* (with all the expected bad days and fallibility) *is about wanting and learning to be an effective teacher*.

DESCRIPTIVE FEEDBACK TO ENCOURAGE STUDENTS

We all know that people respond to encouragement. However, when we give overly 'global' and ebullient praise to students (especially those who have struggled with learning and teachers' authority at school) they may well not believe it. Praise such as, 'That's fantastic great/marvellous/wonderful/brilliant!' – because a student has done a few sentences or remembered to *sit* on the mat (without rolling, pushing or touching) may see them reject such praise and become even more attentional in their behaviour.

When giving encouragement and feedback it is important to have a modicum of *joie de vivre* while at the same time keeping the emphasis on descriptive feedback by affirming what the student has *done* (in work, attitude or behaviour). The focus then is on affirming the student's effort (or at least the direction of their effort!).

'You remembered to start straight away Craig. You've already answered those first two questions. How do you think you'll go on those decimal fractions in questions 4 and 5? Remember the rule about the decimal point and multiplying by 10. I'll come back and see how you're doing later.'

For example, if a student has remembered to use his 'inside voice' (in class-work time), his teacher will *quietly* affirm, acknowledge and describe: 'You remembered to use your inside voice Sean. It makes it so much easier for everyone to work when we use our inside voices.' (This to a grade 3 student on a behaviour plan emphasising a quieter 'working voice' or 'partner-voice' in class-work time.) The teacher will then re-engage the student within his task focus: 'How's your writing going?'

It is also important not to devalue descriptive affirmation by qualifying it: '*Why* can't you do that all the time?' '*If* you only put your hand up like that all the time we would have a much happier class, wouldn't we?' – '*But* you could have done much better *if only* you had …'

CONVEYING EMPATHY

All the students in these studies responded to their teachers' empathy – not feeling sorry for the child but being aware of, and responding to, the child's perspective; giving them a voice (even a basic 'right of reply' in a detention!) and valuing their voice. Empathy is what a child sees in us, hears in us and senses in us over time. It is always more than words. It is about our characteristic manner and tone as we relate to them; not what we say as a result of 'the bad day syndrome'. Children are almost always forgiving of our bad days.

Branwhite (1988) notes that it is a teacher's empathy that is the most valued teacher quality cited by pupils (in Kyriacou, 1991).

KEEPING A SENSE OF HUMOUR

In every study I've read on what students like and positively respond to in their teachers, 'a sense of humour' is always in the top five.[1] This does not mean telling jokes *as such*, it is the ability to see the lighter side of life. We are, after all, stuck in that small classroom space, hour after hour, day after day. We know that laughter can help lift the spirit, reframe tension, even assist stress and coping in positive ways:[2] repartee, *bon mots*, dry wit, irony, farce (plenty of that in schools) and even satire.

In the one-to-one modelling we often engage in with children with EBD; the teacher's 'acting out' of the student's disruptive behaviour often occasions healthy laughter (p 37). Effective teachers, while clearly jaded at times from working with overly challenging students, do not resort to labelling, sarcasm, put-downs, cheap shots or point scoring. When teachers use sarcasm they are seeking to 'score' off a child's behaviour, temperament or personality. Humour is all about defusing tension, or at least reframing the tension so we're less stressed and so are the students. We do not use humour to hurt, whatever the temptation.

GIVING STUDENTS A VOICE THROUGH CLASSROOM MEETINGS

This is a recurrent practice used by teachers throughout this book. They believe that the forum and process of classroom meetings gives a 'voice' to students as individuals; as members of a *classroom group*. Such meetings need to have structure and fair rules to enable that 'voice' to be heard and engaged (see Chapter 5).

These meetings can also assist a class group to understand, even empathise, with a classmate who presents with EBD. I have seen this countless times myself when conducting classroom meetings to address the behaviour of an individual (or several students) in the context of the group (see also Rogers, 2003a).

Such meetings need skilled leadership if they are to work towards the aims envisaged. One of the common uses of classroom meetings is the 'fresh start process' for a hard-to-manage class group. The classroom meeting format often gives the class that has drifted into poor (often unreflective) patterns of behaviour its proper voice; as a means to a 'fresh start' (see p 59, p 68). In such cases, however, it is normally advisable that the class or subject teacher conduct the meeting(s) with a supportive colleague (who also knows, and has the respect of the class).

BALANCING THE SHORT TERM WITH LONGER-TERM AIMS

As noted earlier (p 16) there are many factors we cannot control in the lives of our children. Even while they are with us at school we cannot simply 'control' the behaviour of these children for good; we can lead, guide, expect, even confront (where necessary), but we cannot simply 'make' them behave well or learn well.

In the short term, the many emotional moments in a busy lesson, we will need to both encourage and correct our students. It is in the longer term, however, that teachers normally build up any lasting success regarding behaviour changes.

From the after-class chats (week one), to *supportive* use of time-out, we convey that:

> *While we will not – cannot – allow you to hold the learning and safety of other students to ransom, we will always (beyond time-out, detention and other consequences) support you to make better choices about your behaviour while you are with us here.*

The teachers writing here made a difference because they gave time to the student *beyond* the classroom context. This is noted over and over again by these teachers. In the classroom context children seek to 'belong' – and most do so in co-operative, considerate ways. But the children noted in this book often seek inappropriate, highly attentional or challenging ways to meet the need to belong to their social grouping (in a school context).

These teachers made time (away from the peer audience) to help the child understand their behaviour and come to terms with this need to belong. They helped these students to believe that this need could be met in positive ways. This is where the individual plans (noted in Chapter 3) are often a much more effective *longer-term* support for the children than short-term discipline and consequences alone. What the children themselves note most strongly, however, is the fact that their teacher cares enough to spend this time, this attention, this care and this support – one-to-one with them.

Whenever we spend such time on any supportive strategy we need to distinguish it from 'consequential' time (e.g. time-out, detentions, withdrawal of privileges). Due consequences are essential in a school behaviour policy but they also – always – need to be balanced by longer-term *support*.

Caveat

All long-term support is costly; it is labour intensive. Many teachers (at primary level) spend a lot of non-contact time supporting children with behaviour and learning. Beyond any natural whingeing these teachers always say it was worth it.

Key principles and practices

▶ Appreciating the critical nature of *consistent* colleague support.

▶ Establishing whole-school approaches, providing 'structures' within relationships.

▶ Being persistently willing to persist, coupled with holding an unflagging respect for the child.

▶ Accepting fallibility in ourselves and others – acknowledging 'bad day syndrome'.

▶ Separating the behaviour from the person.

▶ Focusing on the child's efforts towards change.

▶ Keeping the focus on the 'primary' behaviour or issue.

▶ Developing key discipline skills.

▶ Using our leadership power *for* and *with* our children.

▶ Using descriptive feedback to encourage.

▶ Conveying empathy to our students.

▶ Keeping a sense of humour.

▶ Giving students a voice through classroom meetings.

▶ Balancing the short term with longer-term aims.

We become more effective as teachers through reflection, within the values, expectations, behaviours, principles, goals and skills we hold relative to concepts like 'effective' or 'good'.

In this sense it is not mere utility that drives us; we are purpose-driven as well as needs-driven. Based on the fundamental values of mutual respect, mutual regard and the dignity of the individual we seek to be 'a good teacher' – we reflect (from time to time) on what such 'effectiveness' and 'goodness' might mean for us. The teachers writing here have reminded us about what good (and fallible and tired) teachers are like and why.

Aristotle (in his Nichomachean Ethics) *makes the point that 'of every art' we become 'good or bad as a result of building well ...' and: ...this makes it our duty to see that our activities have the right character, since the differences of quality in them are repeated in the dispositions that follow in their train. So it is a matter of real importance whether our early education confirms us in one set of habits or another. It would be nearer to the truth to say that it makes a very great difference indeed, in fact all the difference in the world.*[3]

ENDNOTES

1. McInerney, D.M. and McInerney, V. (1994); Rogers, B. (2002).
2. Rogers, B. (2003) (pp 114–115) Nash (1968) suggests that humour can help a person 'to some extent deal with his repressed emotions'. This may well be true of the group as well. (Ibid. p. 117.) Malcolm Muggeridge reminds us that 'We can bear to be human because, as humans, we can laugh.' (in Nicholas Bentley's How Can You Bear to be Human, Penguin, 1957 p. 10). Frank Muir has noted that 'essentially laughter is a kindly human characteristic' (in his preface to the Oxford Book of Humorous Prose).
3. Aristotle's *Nichomachean Ethics* Book Two, Chapter One. In J.A.K. Thompson's translation (Penguin Classics, 1953, p. 56).

7

Narratives: How Teachers' Stories Connect Us, Support Us, Encourage Us and Enable Us as Teachers

Sharn Hatch

Sharn Hatch has written a thought-provoking essay on narratives in the teaching profession: their place, their purpose, their effect. Sharn's essay encourages us to consider the place of reflection inherent in the narrative journey. Such reflection within – and from the narrative – enables us to gain meaning from what happens to us as we interact with, and teach, our children. Such stories further enable our professional encouragement and growth.

STORIES

Stories have surrounded us from our earliest years. They have formed the warp and woof of the fabric of our lives. As children we sat in silent rapture as we were transported to another time and place by the stories of our culture and cultures less familiar. For some, it was Sunday School stories of floods, famines and a baby born in a manger. For others, it was stories of conquerors and heroes, goblins and ghouls. These stories enriched our imaginations and added to the storehouse of our knowledge. Now, as adults, the narratives of movies, television shows, books and magazines, advertisements, photos and news reports become our daily reality. We have formed the stories that we have told, and those stories have formed us. They have become us and we have become them. Like the Borg in the television story, *Star Trek*, we are assimilated.

The purpose of this essay is to provide a framework by which to understand and reflect on the stories in this book. I draw particularly upon the work of Stephen Preskill (1998) who has identified five narrative types. Bruner (1996) maintains that there is one prime rule for all narratives. He suggests that there should be a reason for it that distinguishes it from silence. Preskill's narrative types provide five reasons why the silence is broken by teachers' stories. The following reflects on some of the stories in this book in terms of Preskill's five narrative types. I also draw upon the stories that surround us in our world to explain and exemplify these narrative types.

NARRATIVES AS REPRESENTATIONS OF REALITY

Jerome Bruner (1996) acknowledges the link between ourselves and our stories. He suggests that narratives are representations of reality. They are not merely fabricated stories meant to amuse or entertain, but are encapsulated fragments of what people find real and meaningful in their worlds. It is as Bartlett explains, 'People are still longing for a story because they are still longing for meaning' (in Wall, 2000, p. 1). In this sense narratives are active and not just passive retellings of events gone by. They are a way of making meaning out of the experiences of everyday life, of visualising the world, organising the past and explaining the present. They help one identify, create and justify one's place in the world.

As the embodiment of beliefs, values, fears, hopes and dreams, narratives become precious and meaningful. They are one's private experiences of the world. When narrating these stories, that private world becomes a public utterance (Cohen and Shires, 1988). In sharing their stories the teachers in this book not only mediate their private experiences to make them publicly known, but also proffer themselves. As such, their stories are precious. They are gifts offered in trust. In each of these teachers' narratives they paint a picture of who they are, what they deem important and how they relate to the world. In Langellier's words, 'in a most profound way, our stories tell us who we are and who we can – or cannot – be, at both surface and deep level meaning' (1989, p. 267)

NARRATIVES AS REPRESENTATIONS OF CULTURE

As well as being a vehicle for the presentation of self, each story expresses an element of the teaching culture. They are, as Bruner (1996) declares, signposts to what is culturally relevant. They provide a window through which one can glimpse the teacher's world and contribute to an understanding of what it takes to be a good teacher. Preskill (1998) acknowledges this. He offers that teachers narratives are guides to the challenges, adversities and wonders of educating children and that each narrative offers a vicarious experience of life in the classroom:

> *The protagonists in these narratives grapple with all of the difficulties that make teaching in contemporary schools so daunting, but their stories highlight the imagination and commitment of teachers who see possibility in the most trying of circumstances. They reaffirm the role that teachers can play in humanising and democratising students and in unleashing their ability to make a difference in the world.* (p 1)

While teachers' narratives are of general public interest, practising and pre-service teachers especially respond to narratives of the classroom. This is particularly true of pre-service teachers who thirst for 'real' classroom stories. These stories encourage and fuel their sense of purpose and provide them with an experience of the classroom, however vicarious. For the veteran teacher, these stories are vehicles through which they can interconnect and reflect on their own practice.

TYPES OF NARRATIVE

Preskill's five narrative types are essentially the identification of five different 'plots'. A plot is the result of action taken in regard to events. Actions have reasons and what people do does not happen by chance. Beliefs, thoughts, values, desires and theories motivate their actions. A narrative combines motivated action in response to an event to form a 'plot'. Preskill's work on teachers' stories is valuable in understanding the motivated actions which keep the teacher coming to work five days a week, 42 weeks a year.

Bourdieu (1991) would refer to teachers' stories as their cultural capital. They are the wealth that teachers possess in the form of their knowledge, ideas, attitudes and values. Preskill has categorised this cultural capital into five particular types of narratives:

▶ the narrative of social criticism
▶ the narrative of apprenticeship
▶ the narrative of reflective practice
▶ the narrative of journey
▶ the narrative of hope.

Not all narratives fit neatly into a particular category. Some narratives, such as that by Elizabeth McPherson, can be understood on different levels. So the story of Luke is about a teacher's journey of discovery into understanding the mind of a small boy and yet is also a narrative of hope where she expresses a sense of wonder at the life that is being transformed before her eyes (p 9)

NARRATIVE OF SOCIAL CRITICISM

The narrative of social criticism is about redressing an imbalance. This can be socio-economic, racial, gender or ability. Commonly, in Australian teacher-training programmes, pre-service teachers are encouraged to be professionally critical of education systems and practices. This is frequently done through subjects which offer an introductory understanding of education and which critically reflect on the history, practices, culture and aims of education. Preskill observes that pre-service teachers are often unaware of the role that education has played in maintaining social inequities. While they tend to focus on the importance of educating young minds and providing a safe secure environment for intellectual growth, they are often unaware that schools are also places where all children should be valued, respected and given the opportunity to overcome disadvantage.

There are many teachers' narratives in the popular media which critique school and social practices. These narratives of social criticism focus on issues both historical and contemporary that prevent schools from fulfilling their mandate. *To Sir With Love* (Braithwaite, 1959) is a story about a black engineer who is forced to take a job in a rough London school. While the story chronicles Mr Thackery's journey of self discovery, it also investigates the effects of low socio-economic status on life opportunities. This rookie teacher gradually becomes aware of how social circumstances have disadvantaged his students. This knowledge compels him eventually to undertake affirmative action to redress the situation.

The movie *Stand and Deliver* (Menendez, 1988) presents a similar scenario. Mr Escalante is a brilliant and inspirational high school mathematics teacher who motivates and encourages his low achieving, East Los Angeles *barrio* students to overcome social stigma and disadvantage. This story focuses on the assumptions and biases held by mainstream authorities about disadvantaged children. Escalante's compassion for these students motivates them to pass the Advanced Placement Calculus Test – a feat unheard of in the history of the school.

Likewise, in her story, 'Alex wins a race', Karen Kearney (p 27) tells the story of Alex – a young adolescent with learning disabilities and a lack of motivation. It is her insights into Alex's interests and her actions to motivate him that open up a world of opportunities for the Year 6 student. Without her efforts to redress an imbalance, Alex would never have had the opportunity to conquer his fears and 'go for gold'. Narratives of social criticism play an important role in highlighting and supporting the principles of social justice and equity.

NARRATIVE OF APPRENTICESHIP

The narrative of apprenticeship is about teacher discipleship or mentoring. One of the earliest examples of this form of narrative is the story of how Jesus Christ trained his twelve disciples to follow in His footsteps. After a three-year apprenticeship period of studying his methods and pedagogy, these 12 men then undertook their own teaching ministry. Without their teacher's support and encouragement, these 12 men would not have gone on to change philosophical and theological thought in the Western world.

Similarly, pre-service teachers in their university-based lessons are exposed to the theories and practices of schools. While this is deemed valuable, it is also recognised that field training is essential. Throughout their training period pre-service teachers are stationed with an experienced practising teacher in an attempt to be apprenticed into the system. While most Australian universities continue to adopt the two to three weeks per semester practicum, others have recognised the value of prolonged exposure to real teachers in real classrooms and have adopted internship programmes. These 'interns' are stationed with an experienced teacher for a complete semester and gain the invaluable experience of day-to-day life in the classroom over a complete school term.

Louanne Johnson's (1993) autobiography has elements of this form of narrative. Louanne's story is that of another 'neophyte' teacher being challenged by unruly and riotous high school students. She relates her trials and tribulations as she seeks to conquer their rebellion and fire their enthusiasm. It is partially through the nurturing, support and encouragement of co-workers that she finds the strength and motivation to continue in her efforts. Narratives of apprenticeship are valuable as they explicate the teacher's journey from novicehood to effective practitioner.

NARRATIVE OF REFLECTIVE PRACTICE

The narrative of reflective practice is inherent within all teachers' stories. Teachers are, or should be, reflective. The importance of being a reflective practitioner is emphasised throughout pre-service training. Trainee teachers are required to examine and critique their practice, their thinking and their effectiveness. While this skill is nurtured and fostered in teacher training institutions, it is in the field that this skill is fully developed. The practising teacher engages in reflection throughout the school day: in how their lessons are planned, implemented and evaluated; in how they interact with the children, staff and parents; and in how effective and socially just they are. It is through this reflective practice that the teacher identifies inadequacies and improves their practice. This is particularly evident in Louanne's story. She continually reflects on her inadequate teaching practices and inability to gain the attention of the class. Being aware that these students will not respond to conventional teaching and behaviour management strategies, she adopts an unconventional approach that is particularly student centred.

The stories in this book are all narratives of reflection. Larry Taylor's story about Tom (p 24) is an illustration of teacher reflection in practice. Larry contemplates the strategy he used to understand the animosity that had developed between himself and his student. It is careful reflection on the child's response to the strategy and his own willingness to take a risk that enables Larry to come to a more complete understanding of their relationship. Likewise Elizabeth McPherson's story of Luke (p 9) demonstrates the cognitive processes that a teacher continually engages in to understand the complexities of a child. It was the dawning realisation that fear and insecurity were driving forces in Luke's life that prompted Elizabeth to modify her attitude and behaviour towards this child.

NARRATIVE OF JOURNEY

The narrative of reflection is also evident in the narrative of journey, for without reflection, growth and change cannot occur. These narratives are autobiographical and highlight how the teacher grows and changes throughout their years of teaching. These narratives will frequently express the highs and lows; the trials and tribulations of teaching as the teacher comes to a new understanding of their role as they travel along the path of their teaching journey.

'The Global Classroom' by Peter D'Angelo (p 12) is representative of this form of narrative. It speaks of his journey as a new language teacher in the suburbs of multicultural Melbourne. As we follow along in his journey we witness his struggles to communicate with the students, and his growing revelation of his own prejudices and assumptions. His journey as a teacher became a journey of self discovery.

While Peter's story is evidently one of journey, the narratives already mentioned also depict journeys travelled. Mr Thackery's journey of discovery in *To Sir With Love* (Braithwaite, 1959) involves learning some enduring lessons about his sense of commitment and the value of people and relationships. For Elizabeth, her journey entailed an understanding of the meaning of love and compassion.

NARRATIVE OF HOPE

The fifth of Preskill's narrative types is the 'narrative of hope'. This narrative, 'accentuates optimism and imagination and a sense of wonder as foundations for good education' (p. 10). Pre-service teachers commonly have a sense of wonder about the teaching profession. Their idealism and exuberance is evident in their discussions and classroom activities. It is folklore that as the young recruit becomes more entrenched in the system, this idealism and wonder gives way to cynicism and pragmatism. Practising teachers who still evince a sense of optimism about their profession are sometimes seen as an anomaly. This cynicism is reflected in teachers' practice and expectations for their students.

Robin Williams' role as John Keating in *Dead Poets Society* (Weir, 1989) is an example of a 'teacher anomaly'. Although he is surrounded by conservatism and ingrained practice, he embodies all that is fresh, new and exciting in teaching. He imparts his enthusiasm for learning to his students and encourages them to abandon tradition and venture out into the unknown.

Peter D'Angelo, too, evinces a narrative of hope. His story captures a sense of optimism and enthusiasm. Even after many years of teaching his belief in the value of education as a life-changing force is evident. He notes that education is about instilling dignity and worth and from his words we can gather that he sees this as the noblest of pursuits.

TO CONCLUDE

Stephen Preskill's five narrative types provide a valuable tool for analysing teachers' narratives. The stories in this book appear, at first reading, to be simple reflections of life in the classroom. However, through applying his framework, it becomes apparent that the stories deal with disparate and various aspects of a teacher's life, work and relationships.

The particular narratives in this book have provided insight into the lives and cultures of our teachers. Whatever the narrative, be it that of social criticism, hope, journey, reflection or apprenticeship, these stories have offered a glimpse into what is important and valuable in the lives of our educators.

First and foremost, teachers are people, but it is their evident commitment to service and their ability to reflect on who they are and what they do that differentiates them. This ability to reflect ensures that teachers are and will continue to be agents of change. These stories tell of the lives that have been touched and changed. As Bill Rogers notes in his contribution, 'We can't predict where our children may end up' (p 1). Who knows where these individuals have trod and what impact they have had in society. And while we can but wonder about Alex, Luke, Trung, Rebecca, Talia or Tom, those teachers who have touched their lives can know that in some small way, they made a difference.

Conclusion

The nineteenth century novelist George Eliot (Mary Ann Evans) was once asked if she was a pessimist or an optimist.

'I am neither,' came the reply, 'I am a meliorist.' (cited in Potter, 1950)

In re-reading these essays – and reflecting on them yet again – I suspect that this might be the settled response of the teachers here. We are 'meliorists'.

I know I am a 'meliorist' – someone who believes that the world (and our little bit of it: Jason, Dean, Bilal, Tran, Melissa, Rebecca ... 4C, 8D, 10E ...) *may be improved by persistent, practical, human effort.*

Each of these teachers has enabled their students to feel special, to feel positive and more secure about themselves and their place in their world. They have encouraged their students to see the best in themselves and have sought to enable them as learners to take conscious and thoughtful control of their learning and behaviour.

These teachers showed continuing respect and liking for their students even in the face of difficult, challenging, disruptive and hostile behaviours; they didn't give up, or give in. While not ignoring or 'playing down' (or to) their inappropriate and disruptive behaviour they taught their students different and better pathways, gave new options; they gave guidance, direction, support and hope. In these teachers – at least – the young people found adults who believed in them and who helped them belong and grow.

They won't forget these teachers.

In a sense there is no 'conclusion' to a book like this. There will always be teachers like these, here, who have shared themselves – and their teaching journey – with us. Thank God (literally) that there are teachers like this in our schools. I hope their accounts will continue to encourage the kind of teaching they have shared with us.

Appendix

Nick's individual behaviour management plan

Musgrave Hill State School

NICK'S GOAL BEHAVIOURS

- ▶ Follow teacher's directions
- ▶ Work quietly on task
- ▶ Keep hands and feet to self
- ▶ To use the computer only when given permission

ACKNOWLEDGEMENTS FOR NICK'S GOAL ACHIEVEMENT

- ▶ Whole class acknowledgement system (personal points/group points)
- ▶ Each smiley face = 1 stamp
- ▶ 10 stamps = 15 minutes computer or time in Middle Brumby 30 minutes

PROACTIVE STRATEGIES

1. Breakfast programme:
   Mum takes scooter to classroom and Nick goes straight to the office for breakfast and his medication.
2. Family is seeking interagency support.
3. Ring Nanny with good news or to calm himself down with her.
4. Modified programme – attached. Collegial support from Support Teacher Learning Difficulties, Middle Brumby and Junior Stage Teachers.
5. Learning support assistance.
6. Chaplain/Counsellor (Rock and Water programme).
7. Seasons Programme – issues from parents' divorce.
8. Use computer for writing because of fine motor issue.
9. Chill out place – in reading corner by his own choice.
10. Wear glasses.
11. PALS – Positive Approach To Life Situations Programme (Griffith University Gold Coast Programme).
12. Teach class to ignore his inappropriate behaviour.

13. Build in time with Junior Stage reading teacher from 10–10.30 am.
14. Allow take up time.
15. Mother has agreed to respond to phone calls from school.

CONSEQUENCES PLAN

Re-issue direction:
'Nick you need to (e.g. keep your hands and feet to yourself).' Allow take up time by moving away and doing something else for a minute.

Complies: 'Good choice Nick. Well done.' (Reinforce with smiley face for following directions.)

Does not comply: 'Nick, you have chosen not to (e.g. keep your hands and feet to yourself). You are now on Marker 1.'

NICK

Day: Date:	FOLLOW TEACHER DIRECTION	WORK QUIETLY ON TASK	KEEP HANDS AND FEET TO SELF	USING COMPUTER WITH PERMISSION	STAMPS	ACKNOWLEDGEMENTS RECEIVED
9.00	☐	☐	☐	☐	=	
9.30	☐	☐	☐	☐	=	
10.00	☐	☐	☐	☐	=	
10.30	☐	☐	☐	☐	=	
11.40	☐	☐	☐	☐	=	
12.10	☐	☐	☐	☐	=	
12.40	☐	☐	☐	☐	=	
1.50	☐	☐	☐	☐	=	
2.20	☐	☐	☐	☐	=	

First Session: 9.00, 9.30, 10.00, 10.30

Second Session: 11.40, 12.10, 12.40

Third Session: 1.50, 2.20

*10 stamps = 15min on the computer or 30 min in Middle Brumby

I have had this document explained to me and I agree with the contents.
Date _____

_____   _____   _____   _____
(PARENT)   (STUDENT)   (ADMINISTRATION)   (CLASS TEACHER)

There is always a way back.

1. Inappropriate behaviour continues – direction and choice given.

2. Inappropriate behaviour continues – move to Reading Corner. // S re-enters by saying, I'm ready to come back now.

3. Inappropriate behaviour continues – ring deputy principal, student to deputy principal.

4. Inappropriate behaviour continues – Parent informed.

5. Total refusal to comply or aggression – removal of S to admin or removal of class and teacher using red card system. Repair and rebuild. Parent informed.

Inappropriate behaviour – direction given – Where are you? Where do you want to be? How do you find your way back?

Appropriate behaviour in the classroom – positive reinforcement system.

On Marker 1
'Nick, you are on Marker 1. You have the choice to (e.g. keep your hands and feet to yourself) or go to Marker 2, which is Reading corner for 5 minutes.'

Complies: 'Good choice Nick. Well done.' (Reinforce with smiley face for following directions.)
Does not comply: 'Nick, you have chosen not to (keep your hands and feet to yourself). You are showing me that you have chosen Reading Corner.'

On Marker 2
'Nick, you need to go quietly to the Reading Corner. This is a thinking time to help you make better choices. If you cannot do that I will need to ring Mrs Smart, and she will ring your mother.'

Complies: After Nick has settled, encourage him, 'Well done for going to the Reading Corner.' Nick sits quietly for 5 minutes. The timer will ring when the 5 minutes is up. Nick returns to his work.
Does not comply: 'Nick you are showing me that I need to ring Mrs Smart. You need to go to the office.'

On Marker 3
Complies: Nick goes to the office.
Does not comply: Ring Mrs Smart who will advise mother of Nick's behaviour.

On Marker 4
Complies: Nick goes to the office.
Does not comply: Mother will be phoned again to collect Nick.

RE ENTRY:

From Reading Corner: – own choice
                               – no comments made.
From Mrs Smart/Mr Marsh: after a session – Nick needs to say 'I'm ready to go back.'
                                                  – Teacher to acknowledge by giving a nod.
                                                  – No verbal comment – no judgement – no emotion.

SUMMARY OF CONSEQUENCES PLAN:

Re-issue direction
Marker 1   Last warning
Marker 2   Time-out (5 min) in the classroom
Marker 3   Time-out in office and phone call to parent
Marker 4   Another phone call to parent and Nick collected to go home
If necessary suspension or exclusion will be implemented.

Class Teacher   **Student**
Parent   **Parent**
D. Principal

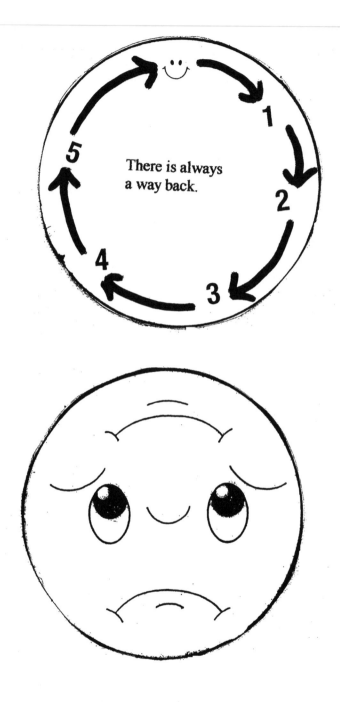

Nick's individual behaviour management plan

Nick's Timetable – 2001 (Term 2)   * Collegial Support

TIME	MONDAY	TUESDAY	WEDNESDAY	THURSDAY	FRIDAY
8:50 AM	**Student of the Week**	...Morning Session (carpet)...			**Jobs**
9:00 AM	Homework (Whole class) – pass out sheet Modelled reading	Homework – Group 2 Drop Everything & Read – Group 3 – swap above after 15 min	* Bushwalking with Middle Brumby 9:00–12:00	*AbraKIDazzle with Middle Brumby 9:00–12:00	Homework – Group 2 Peer Testing/DEAR – Grp 3 – swap above after 15 min Whole Class Dictation
9:30AM	Reading Rotations Group A guided reading Other groups – reading arm	Reading Rotations Group B guided reading Other groups– reading arm			Reading Rotations Group D guided reading Other groups – reading arm
10:00 AM	Maths – Number Study	*10:00–10:30 Peer support with juniors (with Mrs Shaw) 10:30–11:00 Maths – Theme			Class Meeting (even week) or Music (10:15) (odd week)
11:00 AM		ABC –Mar	*MORMING TEA* Adv. Playground – Mar		
11:40 AM	Positive Approach to Life Situations	LOTE			*Peer support with juniors (with Mrs Shaw)
12:10 PM	Word Block – dictation – lesson –chart/MI activity	Word Block – Chart/MI activity	12:10–1:10 *With Mrs. Prouten (provide set work)	Religion	Interschool Sport
12:40 PM	Writing Block	Writing Block		*Learning Support Lesson With Mrs. Shaw	
1:10 PM	ABC – Mar		*LUNCH*		
1:50PM	Integrated Unit	Integrated Unit	Integrated Unit	*Rock and Water	Interschool Sport

Bibliography

Adler, A. (1957) *Understanding Human Nature*. New York : Fawcett.

Aurelius, M. (1980) *The Meditations of Marcus Aurelius* (Trans. G. Long). Grolier, Connecticut: The Harvard Classics.

Bourdieu, P. (1991) *Language and Symbolic Power* (Trans. G. Raymond & M. Adamson). Cambridge: Polity Press.

Braithwaite, E. R. (1959) *To Sir With Love*. London : Bodley Head.

Breheney, C., Mackrill, V. and Grady, N. (1996) *Making Peace at Mayfield: A Whole-School Approach to Behaviour Management*. (Armadale) Melbourne: Eleanor Curtain Publishers.

This is a book I would strongly encourage colleagues to purchase when they are addressing challenging students and classes within a whole-school approach. This is a book of hope about a school that decided to make a difference in a demanding and difficult social environment where hostility, suspicion, poor communication, conflict – even violence – was a recurrent pattern. It shows how a whole-school approach can and does work.

Bruner, J. (1996) *The Culture of Education*. Cambridge: Harvard University Press.

Cohen, S. and Shires, L. M. (1988) *Telling Stories: A Theoretical Analysis of Narrative Fiction*. London: Routledge.

Cooper, P. (1997b) The reality and hyperreality of AD/HD and educational and cultural analysis. In P. Cooper and K. Ideus (eds.), *Attention Deficit/Hyperactivity Disorder: Medical, Educational and Cultural Issues* (1997, 2nd revised edition). East Sutton: The Association of Workers for Children with Emotional and Behavioural Difficulties.

Coopersmith, S. (1967) *The Antecedents of Self-Esteem*. San Francisco : Freeman.

Crawford, D., Bodine, R. and Hoglund, R. (1993) *The School for Quality Learning*. Champaign, Illion: Research Press.

Dreikurs, R. (1968) *Psychology in the Classroom: A Manual For Teachers* (2nd edition). New York: Harper and Row.

Dreikurs, R., Grunwald, B. and Pepper, F. (1982) *Maintaining Sanity in the Classroom* (2nd edition.). New York: Harper and Row.

Erickson, E. (1970) *Identity, Youth and Crisis*. London: Norton Press.

Ginott, H. (1971) *Teacher and Child: A Book for Parents and Teachers*. New York: Macmillan.

Gillborn, D., Nixon, J. and Ruddock, J. (1993) *Dimensions of Discipline: Rethinking Practice in Secondary Schools*. London: Her Majesty's Stationery Office.

Glasser, W. (1986) *Control Theory in Classrooms*. New York: Harper and Row.

Glasser, W. (1992) *The Quality School*. New York: Harper Collins.

Howell, K. (1993) Eligibility and need: is there a difference in being disturbed and being disturbed? In S. Richardson, and J. Izard. (eds.) *Student Behaviour Problems: Positive Initiatives and New Frontiers*. Hawthorn, Victoria: ACER Press.

Johnson, L. (1993) *My Posse Don't Do Homework*. New York: Saint Martin's Press.

Kyriacou, C. (1986) *Effective Teaching in Schools*. Oxford: Basil Blackwell.

Kyriacou, C. (1991) *Essential Teaching Skills*. London: Basil Blackwell

Langellier, K. M. (1989) Personal narratives: Perspectives on theory and research. *Text and Performance Quarterly*, 9, pp243–276.

McInerney, D.M. and McInerney, V. (1998) *Educational Psychology – Constructing Learning* (2nd edition). Sydney: Prentice-Hall.

McGrath, H. and Francey, S. (1993) *Friendly Kids, Friendly Classrooms*. Melbourne: Longman

Maslow, A. (1972) *Motivation and Personality* (2nd edition). New York: Van Nostrand Reinhold.

Menendez, R. (1988) *Stand and Deliver* [Film]. USA: Warner Brothers.

O'Brien, T. (1998) *Promoting Positive Behaviour*. London: David Fulton Publishers.

Preskill, S. (1998) Narratives of teaching and the quest for the second self. *Journal of Teacher Education*, 49 (5), pp344–357.

Potter, S. (1950) *Our Language*. London: Pelican Books.

Rickard, J. (1994) *Relaxation for Children*. Melbourne: ACER Press.

Robertson, J. (1998) *Effective Classroom Control: Understanding Teacher-pupil Relationships* (3rd edition) London: Hodder and Stoughton.

Rogers, B. (1992) *Supporting Teacher in the Workplace*. Jacaranda Press Milton, Queensland. In the UK (1996) Managing Teacher Stress, Pitman, London.

Rogers, B. (1994) *Behaviour Recovery: A Whole-school Program for Mainstream Schools*. Melbourne: Australian Council for Educational Research.
The revised edition (2003) addresses EBD behaviours and programmes for addressing challenging and EBD behaviours in mainstream and special school settings. This edition includes many photocopiable masters *to enable teachers to draw up plans for a range of distracting and disruptive behaviours from calling out and rolling on the mat to badly handled anger.* In the UK (2004) London: Paul Chapman Publishing.

Rogers, B. (1996) *Managing Teacher Stress*. London: Pitman.

Rogers, B. (1998) *You Know the Fair Rule and Much More: Strategies for Making the Hard Job of Discipline and Behaviour Management in Schools Easier*. Melbourne: Australian Council for Educational Research.

Rogers, B. (2002a) *I Get By With a Little Help: Colleague Support in Schools*. Melbourne : Australian Council for Educational Research.

Rogers, B. (ed.) (2002b) *Teacher Leadership and Behaviour Management*. London: Paul Chapman Publishing.

Rogers, B. (2003a) *Behaviour Recovery: Practical Programs for Challenging Behaviour*. London: Paul Chapman Publishing.

Rosenthal, R. and Jacobson, L. (1986) *Pygmalion in the Classroom*. New York: Holt Rinehart and Winston.

Rosenthal, R. and Jacobsen, L.F. (1967) Teacher expectations for the disavantaged. *Reading from Scientific American*. San Francisco: W.F. Freeman & Co.

Rutter, M., Maughan, B., Mortimer, P. and Ouston, J. (1979) *Fifteen Thousand Hours*. London: Open Books.

Seligman, M. (1991) *Learned Optimism*. Sydney: Random House.

Shaw, G.B. (1965) *Pygmalion*. London: Penguin Books.

Wall, D. (2000) The art of the narrative. *Southern Accents*, 23 (6), pp90–94.

Weir, P. (Director) (1989) *Dead Poets Society* [Film]. USA: Touchstone Pictures.

Wragg, J. (1989) *Talk Sense to Yourself: A Program For Children and Adolescents*. Melbourne: Australian Council for Educational Research.

Index

Author Index

DATE DUE